METHODIST WORSHIP

IN RELATION TO FREE CHURCH WORSHIP

by

JOHN BISHOP, M.A.
Author of
Study Notes on Preaching and Worship

WIPF & STOCK · Eugene, Oregon

Wipf and Stock Publishers
199 W 8th Ave, Suite 3
Eugene, OR 97401

Methodist Worship
In Relation to Free Church Worship
By Bishop, John
Copyright©1950 Methodist Publishing - Epworth Press
ISBN 13: 978-1-5326-3167-2
Publication date 4/25/2017
Previously published by Epworth Press, 1950

Every effort has been made to trace the current copyright
owner of this publication but without success. If you have
any information or interest in the copyright, please contact the publishers.

PREFACE

THIS BOOK is a considerably reduced version of a thesis approved by Bristol University for the degree of Master of Arts. The title of the thesis was 'The Forms and Psychology of Worship in the Free Church Tradition with Special Reference to Methodism'. The sections dealing with the worship of the English Puritans and the renaissance of worship in the Free Churches during the nineteenth century have been omitted in order to keep the size and price of this book within reasonable limits. In recent years a considerable number of books have been published by Churchmen of many denominations on the art of public worship, but there is very little that deals with the origin and development of Methodist worship. It is hoped that this book will supply a need and will encourage others to explore this field more thoroughly. I trust that this book will not only be of interest to the people called Methodists, but to those in other communions who wish to know something of our way of worship. The more we learn about each other's methods of worship, the closer will we be drawn together in understanding and love.

This study is born out of a lifelong interest in the subject, constant experimentation and practice in the Churches where I have ministered, and no little reading, conversation and observation. I am indebted to all who have written on this subject, and some measure of my obligation is acknowledged in the footnotes and the bibliography.

There are several books which have appeared recently which would have been invaluable during the preparation of this book had they appeared earlier. One has not yet been published in this country; it is by Dr. Henry Sloane Coffin: *The Public Worship of God* (Westminster Press, Philadelphia). It is described as a source-book for leaders of services, and is an admirable treatment of the Reformed tradition of worship. For those who wish to study in detail the Free Church tradition of Christian worship in England (excluding Methodism), there is no finer book than *The Worship of the English Puritans*, written by a Congregational minister, Rev. Dr. Horton Davis, and published by the Dacre Press. I would acknow-

PREFACE

ledge the kindness of the author and publishers of this book in allowing me to see the galley proofs while I was preparing my thesis. Dr. W. D. Maxwell's latest book, *Concerning Worship* (Oxford Press) had its origin in lectures given to Canadian Chaplains during the War, and is written from the standpoint of a Scottish Churchman.

Three Methodist authors have recently made valuable contributions in this field of study. Rev. W. F. Flemington in his *The New Testament Doctrine of Baptism* (published by the S.P.C.K.) deals in the concluding chapter with the New Testament baptismal teaching in its relation to the baptism of infants. Dr. J. E. Rattenbury has added to the great debt owed to him by the whole of Methodism by his latest volume, *The Eucharistic Hymns of John and Charles Wesley*, which includes a reprint of the 150 Hymns on the Lord's Supper and Dr. Brevint's Preface. Dr. Leslie F. Church, in *More About the Early Methodist People* (both published by the Epworth Press), devotes the final chapter to a consideration of 'Worship —public and private' which forms a most useful supplement to the brief account given in this book of our distinctive Methodist services.

There are a few friends to whom I am in duty bound to make special acknowledgement for their help: to Dr. A. L. Drummond of Alva for his keen interest, and the loan of books and magazine articles; to members of the Wesley Historical Society and in particular to the Rev. Frederick Hunter for guidance in Wesley literature; to Rev. Nolan B. Harmon, Jnr., and Dr. Oscar T. Olson for the loan of books and for information about Methodist worship, both past and present, in the United States; to Rev. Dr. Arthur Dakin, Principal of Bristol Baptist College, for his supervision of my studies while preparing my thesis, and to the Rev. Frank H. Cumbers the Book Steward, and the publishers for their kind help in preparing the book for publication.

JOHN BISHOP.

ACKNOWLEDGEMENTS

THE AUTHOR and publisher are indebted to the following for kind permission to quote from their copyright works.
Every effort has been made to observe copyright, but in a few instances we have been unable to trace the source; if in these and any other instances we have unwittingly infringed copyright, it is hoped that we shall be pardoned and informed of our mistake:

James Clarke & Co. Ltd. for an extract from *The Presbyter* (see p. 99); and T. and T. Clark for lines from *Our Heritage in Public Worship*, by Dr. Hislop (p. 55), and *Christian Institutions*, by Dr. Allen (p. 57).

Hodder and Stoughton Ltd. for lines from *The Church and the Kingdom*, by Dr. James Denney (p. 50); *The Public Worship of God*, by J. R. P. Sclater (p. 61), and *The Apostolic Preaching and its Developments* by Professor C. H. Dodd (p. 69).

Longmans Green & Co. Ltd. for lines from *Collected Papers*, by Evelyn Underhill (p. 157).

James Nisbet & Co. Ltd. for lines from Dr. Farmer's *Servant of the Word* (p. 51), and *Worship*, by Evelyn Underhill (pp. 11, 20, 30, 153).

Oxford University Press for extracts from *Autobiography*, by Mark Rutherford (p. 38).

S.C.M. Press for lines from *The Creed of a Christian*, by Dr. Nathanael Micklem (p. 64).

CONTENTS

PREFACE iii
ACKNOWLEDGEMENTS v

Introduction

1. THE TWO TYPES OF WORSHIP—CATHOLIC AND EVANGELICAL, OBJECTIVE AND SUBJECTIVE . 1
2. THE HISTORIC EVOLUTION OF FREE CHURCH WORSHIP 8

Part One
The Form and Order of Public Worship in the Free Churches

PRAISE 17
PRAYERS 27
THE LESSONS 41
THE SERMON 46
THE SACRAMENTS 55

Part Two
The Methodist Church—A Detailed Survey of Its Worship

ITS ORIGIN AND DEVELOPMENT 78
DISTINCTIVE METHODIST SERVICES . . . 100
THE METHODIST DOCTRINE OF BAPTISM . . 111
THE METHODIST DOCTRINE OF HOLY COMMUNION . 121
HYMNS IN METHODIST WORSHIP . . . 138

EPILOGUE 154
BIBLIOGRAPHY 159
INDEX OF AUTHORS 163
INDEX OF SUBJECTS 165

Introduction

I. THE TWO TYPES OF WORSHIP—CATHOLIC AND EVANGELICAL, OBJECTIVE AND SUBJECTIVE

THE revival of interest in the theory and practice of public worship is a hopeful sign. There is an urgent need to think through an office of worship in its entirety. An attempt must be made to answer such questions as: What is the purpose of a service of worship? What is the meaning of its rituals and symbols and sacraments? For a religion is judged by its worship, and the Church's life depends upon its worship. Worship is the Church's characteristic action. It is the one thing that the Church alone does, the essential mark of the fellowship of Christ. What keeps Christianity alive in the world is the worshipping community of Christians—which means in practice the local congregation. Worship is an end in itself, and if it is regarded as instrumental to anything else it is not truly worship. The contemplation and adoration of God is the end of human life. Prayers, meditations, Communions, attendance at the services of the Church should be so many moments of concentrated worship in a life which is, in its essential quality, all worship. St. Ignatius Loyola based the whole of his 'Spiritual Exercises' on one truth: 'Man was created for this end—to praise, reverence, and serve the Lord his God.' Where there is no vision of God there can be no real worship.

There are certain principles upon which Christian people are agreed. They are agreed that in worship man brings his offering to God, and whether the offering is thought of in terms of priestly sacrifice or as the homage of 'a broken and contrite heart', it is a duty each man owes to his Creator. They are also agreed that worship is a means of grace. When men worship in spirit and in truth something happens to them. The mind is illumined and secret things are revealed. Burdens are removed or grace to carry them is received. The peace that passes understanding possesses the heart.

Christians are agreed, further, that worship is a testimony to the world of the faith that is in them, a witness that is of particular importance at a time when many are becoming indifferent to the claims of religion. It is not only common worship that is offered, but public worship. It is a social as well as a religious duty.

But to pass beyond the first principles is to pass to differences and apparent confusion. There is little in common between the High Mass of the Roman Catholic, the preaching service of the Methodist, and the silence of the Friends' Meeting. The diversity of human nature makes it impossible that all temperaments should be satisfied with the same religious forms. The apparent confusion can be ultimately reduced to two main types—the priestly and the prophetic. One is distinguished by the prominence of the altar, and other by the prominence of the pulpit. One is popularly called 'Catholic', the other 'Protestant', or perhaps better, 'Evangelical'. The first makes a strong appeal to the natural man and is never likely to be eradicated. The other meets a real and deep need and seems to be necessary to the maintenance of pure religion.

It is frequently assumed that the second type came into existence at the Reformation. It would be wiser to connect it with the prophetic religion of the Old Testament, which was so often in conflict with the priestly. It is not accurate to regard this as a conflict between the essentially good and the essentially bad. It was part of the eternal conflict between the reformer and the constitutionalist, the idealist and the legislator. The prophet loved truth and hated pretence and feared no man, but he was apt to destroy more than ought to be destroyed. The priest easily became conventional and even worldly, substituting the form for the reality, but he knew the value of authority, symbol, ritual, and suggestion. But the contrast was not always as sharp as that. There were priests with prophetic qualities and prophets with priestly affinities.

It is equally important to consider the types of worship found in Palestine in the time of our Lord. Priestly religion was represented in the ornate Temple with its many courts and altars and sacrifices, and its twenty-four courses of priests. Everything was as lavish and impressive as men knew how to make it, and while the Temple stood it was regarded as the centre of the national life. But even more significant was the synagogue, which, if too legalistic to be true to the prophetic religion, represented it in its simplicity and intimacy.

The Temple service with its sacrificial cultus was communal, expressing the worship of the nation, whereas the worship of the synagogue was personal and individual. The local religious service of the synagogue gave the Jewish Church something akin to a parochial system and linked the religious life of every village with the central sanctuary. The sacrificial cultus, says Evelyn Underhill, 'was more deeply understood and more reverently performed, because of the background of personal, disciplined, and instructed religion, the constant meditation of the Law, which the synagogues provided'.[1] In the service of the synagogue, for the first time, ordered corporate worship was dissociated from sacrifice, and centred upon the reading and meditation of Scripture.

[1] *Worship*, p. 209 (James Nisbet & Co.)

The synagogue is the ancestor of the countless forms of free evangelical worship based on Scripture reading, preaching, praise, and extempore prayer.

It was from the synagogue and not from the Temple that Christianity extended itself. But the synagogue and the Temple were not rivals in Judaism and caused no conflicting loyalties among the people. Ordinarily the Jew attended the synagogue and rejoiced in its simplicity, but at the great festivals he offered his sacrifice in the Temple. All through New Testament times and as far as we can tell, through the sub-apostolic period, Christian worship retained the characteristics of the synagogue. It was simple, spontaneous, intimate. But by the third century priestly elements manifested themselves, and from that time to the Reformation worship was predominantly of the Temple type. Then the synagogue type reasserted itself and remains to this day.

From this rapid sketch it appears that the forms which are traditional in the Free Churches are not late innovations and are not to be regarded as inferior to the forms popularly called 'Catholic'. While human differences are as great as they are there is a place for both types and they are meant to complement each other. They may even complement one another in the same Churches and services and should do so if a truly catholic worship is to be attained.

The desire to preserve the truth of the Reformation does not justify the Protestant Churches in refusing to learn anything which Catholic worship can teach. Protestantism has a heritage from Catholicism which it ought to treasure. Professor J. B. Pratt in a psychological study called *The Religious Consciousness* has an interesting chapter entitled, 'Objective and Subjective Worship'. The difference between the two types of worship is that the one aims at producing some effect upon God and the other at making some impression on the mind of the worshipper. Catholic worship centres itself on God, while the tendency of Protestant worship is to seek for the improvement of Man. So the Professor argues that objective worship is more prominent in Catholicism and subjective in Protestantism. In the Protestant Church God is everywhere present but nowhere in particular. In the Roman Church He is present everywhere, but also in a particular place, in the consecrated wafer. The Protestant decks the Church with flowers for the people to see. The Catholic lights his candles for the eye of God. The minister intends that God shall hear the words of the service, but also the congregation. So he utters prayer in a loud voice, facing the people. The priest turns his back on the people and whispers his prayers in a voice too low to be heard and in an unfamiliar tongue: to him the size of the congregation does not matter.[2]

Everything in the Catholic cultus is a means to one end: 'to the greater glory of God.' Catholics frequent their churches during the week because they believe that on the altar God is objectively present as nowhere else. The Mass is a sacrifice to God which does not require intelligent following on the part of the people, which must be performed whether worshippers are present or not. Yet the service commands a loyalty and devoutness which few Protestant services achieve. It cannot be altogether explained on the grounds of superstition. It rests upon the assumption that nothing in a man's life is more significant than the offering of himself to God. It is the conviction that in the Mass something happens which matters that gives the service its peculiar power.

Nearly all the details in a Protestant service are planned with the deliberate purpose of producing certain psychological effects on the people. The Protestant is unable to

[2] *Worship*, p. 297.

accept the miracle of the Mass, but he is also unable to find an alternative account of divine reality as concrete and as dramatically moving as the Mass. Protestant worship can never be objective in the Roman or Anglo-Catholic sense, and there is a growing realization that it has become dangerously subjective. The older view of the Bible at least acted as a norm of objectivity. The Bible took its place in the gap which the Reformation made when it deleted the doctrine of transubstantiation. The Scriptures did determine the form and spirit of worship, and had the effect of curbing extreme individualism. 'The fact that Christianity is no longer generally conceived of as "the religion of a Book" while affording welcome release from a mechanical view of inspiration, has opened the flood-gates of subjectivity. Religion is being interpreted in terms of current thought and experience to such an extent that the passing thought of the age is in danger of ousting the Eternal from the foreground of consciousness.'[3]

On what does the weakness of evangelical worship rest? Worship reaches its climax where the congregation obtains an immediate sense of the presence of God. Catholic worship has a climax of this sort, and that is its strength. The Catholic congregation feels God's presence at the moment of the consecration of the elements. The evangelical service with its demand for a deeper and more personal fellowship has to a large extent lacked such a climax, and that is its weakness. All too easily participation in worship is turned into an intellectual attentiveness which apprehends nothing of God's presence. Worship tends to become utilitarian under such conditions, and the minister chooses hymns, prayers, lessons, and sermon with a view to stimulating his people and rousing them to action.

[3] A. L. Drummond, *The Church Architecture of Protestantism*, p. 189.

'The worshipper in the Protestant Church', says J. B. Pratt, 'must be made to feel as the Catholic feels at the Mass, that something is being done—something in addition to the subjective change in his own consciousness. What the Protestant service needs more than anything else is the development of the objective side of its worship.'[4] How is this to be done? Sometimes an attempt has been made to overcome the weakness of evangelical worship by incorporating greater or less parts of the Catholic cultus into the evangelical service. That this does not lead to the goal is plain. What is needed is a stronger expression of the specifically evangelical fellowship with God. Where a believing heart in prayer lays itself open to the Gospel word, there God is at hand, there He is really present, there is true fellowship with God in the evangelical sense.

The secret of effective worship lies in the willingness of the worshipper to forget himself, and the determination of the minister not to obtrude his personality. As Dean Sperry puts it in his book *Reality in Worship*: 'We have only to cease talking about ourselves when we go to church and to begin talking about God and to God to get on the right road.' Throughout the service there should be the conviction that something is going to happen. The people are to meet with God, and God is going to meet with them, and they are going to do something in the presence of God. They are going to bring to God an offering, the offering of their praise and prayer in the communion of all His saints in heaven and on earth; and God is going to speak to them and have dealings with them, and receive their offering and give it a place in the service of His Kingdom. That spirit of expectancy is of the essence of worship in spirit and in truth.

[4] *The Religious Consciousness*, p. 307.

2. THE HISTORIC EVOLUTION OF FREE CHURCH WORSHIP

IT IS WELL that consideration should be given to the contribution of the Free Church tradition to the worship of the Catholic Church. It may be asked if there are not as many traditions as there are Free Churches. The answer is that though there are differences of emphasis and varieties of local practice these are insignificant in comparison with the agreements in principle. The Free Church heritage is that represented by the three main streams of non-episcopal ecclesiastical tradition in Britain —Presbyterian, Independent, and Methodist. The Quakers have a contribution of their own to make, but it is as distinct from the Free Church contribution as it is from that of the Church of Rome.

The Presbyterians and the Independents are primarily indebted to Geneva for the characteristics of their cult. The Methodist practice has always betrayed its different origin, but since the end of the eighteenth century the three have influenced each other in such a way that they share in common sufficient characteristics to constitute a type. The Methodist movement, breaking away from the Church of England, was inevitably influenced by the practice of the older Puritan Dissenting bodies to which it was gravitating. On the other hand, the already existing Dissenting Churches were very strongly influenced by the Evangelical Revival which brought new life and vigour into them.

The forms of Divine Service which ministers of the Free Churches are required to conduct date from the sixteenth century. In spite of considerable differences between them, they all resulted from the effort of the Reformers to revert to the practice of the Church at an earlier and purer period of its history. It was inevitable that the gain achieved by the Reformation should be accompanied by some loss. Any violent break with historic continuity must shatter links with the past which are of value. The Reformation performed a necessary and drastic operation: malignant growths were ruthlessly cut away, but with the diseased tissue much that was healthy was amputated.

No universally accepted order of service has been able to establish itself in the Reformation Churches such as might have restored a sense of unity. The services themselves have suffered much in their beauty and impressiveness. A severely spiritual cult is under a grave disadvantage when unspiritual natures have to be dealt with. It is through the senses that such people are impressed, and it is by symbols that they can most easily apprehend the unseen. A service which is largely composed of verbal teaching makes heavy demands upon the intellect, and calls for more devoutness than is to be met with among average persons. Sometimes Free Church services have been devoid of beauty, plain and severe to the point of ugliness. Yet unattractive as such services may be to the indifferent or the unspiritually-minded, faithful souls will always feel themselves at home in them.

The two great divisions of Protestantism, while one in spirit, differed in the thoroughness with which they strove to reproduce worship as it was believed to be observed in the early days of Christianity. Luther was cautious and conservative in his alterations. He did not desire to break with the customary ways of worship except where they seemed to be inconsistent with the Gospel teaching. He made it plain that he did not wish to introduce a new law in liturgical matters. 'His view of the Word did not involve any fixed or explicit form of worship. So long as the heart of the Word was soundly preserved, he cared little how the faithful in his own communion expressed their devotion, though he pleaded for a reasonable uniformity.'[1]

Luther did not feel it was his duty to produce a liturgy which should be binding. He recognized that varieties of temperament and tradition would find differing ways of worshipping the one God. His conviction was that unless the Word expressly forbade a form of devotion, there was no need to surrender it. So the Lutheran Churches retained much that the Calvinists rejected. Pictures were left on the walls. The crucifix and the lights remained on the holy table. The Gospel and Epistle were still read every Sunday and made obligatory as texts for the weekly sermon. Luther's revision of the Mass, while it dropped everything which implied a sacrificial oblation of the elements, allowed certain of the ancient prayers to remain, along with the versicles, the Kyrie, the Pax Vobiscum, and the Creed.

The Reformed Churches, with a more definite intention to be guided by the New Testament, went somewhat farther. They did not dispense with prepared prayers at the Sunday Services. They retained the recital of the Apostles' Creed in worship. They continued to observe the great festivals of the Christian Year. They no longer celebrated the Lord's Supper every Sunday, but reserved it for special occasions. In other respects, however, they stripped the service of all but the essentials, making it as bare and simple as they could. They banished organs and sacred pictures from their churches, abolished the fixed lessons, and substituted new forms of prayer for the traditional ones.

[1] Moffatt's essay on Luther, *Christian Worship*, ed. Nathanael Micklem, p. 125.

Part One

Form and Order of Public Worship in the Free Churches

ONE source of weakness in the Free Churches of the present day is their failure to recognize clearly the need for a definite form and structure in worship if it is to be a reality. In many cases the services tend to consist of unrelated items. A service to be satisfying calls for the skill of an architect who can adapt structure to function.

Public worship should be so ordered that it will establish such conditions in the minds and hearts of the congregation as are likely to make them most receptive of and responsive to the workings of the Spirit. As Streeter has pointed out, there is of necessity a reciprocal character about the soul's communion with God. There are moments of pure receptivity, and there are other moments of conscious self-expression. 'He who would pray must at one time speak, at another listen. He who would praise must at one time cry aloud, at another contemplate in peaceful adoration. Passivity must alternate with activity, but the passivity must be that of restful attention, not that of inattention.'[1] A form of worship gives a sense of rest, and variety within that form gives a sense of movement.

Worship is essentially formal and its forms are of the essence. They are not trimmings that can be dispensed with. 'Form without spirit is dead, but spirit without form is not capable of living.'[2]

Properly understood, 'form' means, not the outward appearance of a thing, but its very essence, its nature and character.

---

[1] *Concerning Prayer*, p. 266.   [2] R. Will, *Le Culte*, Vol. II, p. 31.

For of the soul the body form doth take;
For soul is form and doth the body make.[3]

What Spenser implies by those familiar words is that form is the inner reality of a thing. 'That which stamps anything with its own identity is its form.'[4] Modern life has lost its conception of form and has become formless, thereby becoming estranged from worship.

Worship deals with man as he is, and because it deals with the 'form' of human life, it must receive formulation. Worship must use 'forms', in the more modern sense of that term, as prescribed usages and customs. But such outward forms have a real relation to the inward essence. They give shape and body to the movement of the spirit.

Public worship without ritual would seem to be impossible. Ritual, in the technical sense implies a prescribed form of words which constitutes a rite; but in common usage, it also covers the employment of ceremonial and symbolism in public worship. It is important to distinguish ritual from ritualism, which signifies the assigning of primary importance to external observance and is synonymous with formality.

No one can dispute the necessity of ritual in corporate worship. It may be ritual reduced to the simplest forms, as with the Friends, but ritual it is. Free Churchmen have a ritual of their own, and many of them are strongly opposed to the slightest departure from it. Bishop Gore made a legitimate point when he said that 'a religious rite is not less material or less necessary because it is simply performed'.

Judgement on what is congruous or incongruous in public worship depends not only on temperament and the tradition in which a man has been trained, but on the fundamental theological ideas underlying the worship.

[3] *Hymn in Honour of Beauty.* [4] D. G. Peck, *Living Worship*, p. 18.

One thing can be said—that when spiritual life languishes, forms multiply, and when spiritually men are most alert they tend to become independent of much ceremony.

Forms of worship have a value in setting before the worshippers the whole faith. Each full act of worship should set forth the whole Gospel of the Incarnate, Crucified, and Risen Lord, and the Church's response of adoration, thanksgiving, confession, and petition. As Dean Sperry puts it: 'A service is an artistic recapitulation of Christian experience: it is an affirmation of that which the Church holds to be permanently valid and true in Christian history as a whole.'[5]

The task of a public office of worship is to give formal expression to God's word to man and man's response to that word. On one of the towers of Bath Abbey there is a carving of Jacob's ladder. That is a symbol of the worship of the Church, in which God's word comes down to man and man's words go up to God. That rhythm runs all through the service.

There is a traditional procedure and movement of the service. This order even in the Free Churches harks back to the Mass of the Catechumens in the Roman service and through that to the synagogue. The quest for novelty for its own sake in the revision of orders of worship offers little hope of better services. It is with a service as it is with poetry or music: the artist displays his skill best if he works within the convention and not in rebellion against it.

It is a much debated question whether the service should confine itself to one idea, with all its parts making their contribution to that idea, or whether it should have a number of independent ideas which supplement one another. A service certainly ought to be a unity leaving at the end one clear and strong impression. It must have

[5] *Reality in Worship*, p. 175.

shape and meaning. But to confine the service to a single idea and to conceive it in a single mood is to run the risk of losing the attention and interest of the congregation. The power of close attention to one idea is limited. Moreover, the service ought to atone for necessary omissions in the preaching. Often the preacher's message may concern a limited aspect of the Christian life or it may deal with a special topic which may interest only a part of the congregation. Then in the rest of the service the leader of the worship should supply what is lacking in the sermon, so that every one present is satisfied spiritually somewhere in the service.

An order of service is demanded by the diversity and the unity of every congregation. Each body of worshippers is diverse, because it contains individuals in every kind of religious need. All these needs ought to be met and an order is essential to that end. Otherwise the leader will impose his mood on the people. But no less important is the unity of the congregation. The object of worship is one and in their movement toward that object all the diverse needs of the people are met.[6]

In the sixth chapter of Isaiah there is a most suggestive pattern for public worship. Here the elements of an ideal worship are set forth in a clear and psychologically convincing order. First, there is the sense of need on the part of the worshipper. This experience came to Isaiah 'in the year that king Uzziah died'. Once in the temple, Isaiah 'saw the Lord sitting upon a throne, high and lifted up'. That is to say, he had a vision of God. The people should be helped to see some vision of God and experience some fresh awakening to the presence of the divine in their lives.

The next thing that happened to Isaiah was that he felt a deep sense of unworthiness and was led to contrition

[6] See J. R. P. Sclater, *The Public Worship of God*, p. 24.

for his sins. This humility and repentance was both individual and social. 'Woe is me, for I am undone; because I am a man of unclean lips and I dwell in the midst of a people of unclean lips: for mine eyes have seen the King, the Lord of hosts.' The leader of worship has so to present the greatness of the spiritual ideal that people will reach out toward it, and in so doing pour contempt on all their pride.

But it is not enough to awaken the mood of confession and penitence. Relief and comfort, cleansing and forgiveness must also be provided. Something in the service should take a coal from off the altar and cleanse the worshipper with purifying power until he knows that his iniquity is taken away and his sin forgiven. Then there will be a new sensitivity to the voice of God, a greater readiness to hear and obey His call, and say: 'Here am I, send me.'

Dean Sperry thinks of the pattern of worship in terms of thesis, antithesis, and synthesis. As thesis, there is the vision of reality. The antithesis is the contrasting human situation. These are resolved in a synthesis of new understanding, including rededication. So he divides the service into three parts. The first is a direct call to worship and the celebration of one of God's attributes. 'This opening part of the service should be broad, simple, familiar and dogmatic.' After this truth has been proclaimed and the worshipper brought into the presence of God there will follow a statement of those aspects of human nature which are suggested in contrast. Once the service has dealt adequately with this contrast and given an assurance of forgiveness it passes on to the thought of rededication. The sermon should clarify and interpret the religious experience as a whole. It should be followed by a hymn, one of service and action. This marks the moment of the worshipper's return to his life in the world. 'If the sermon is dull and inadequate the hymn gives the people the last word. If the sermon is really effective there is still greater reason for giving this final opportunity to the people to express themselves.'

In every service there should be one high moment for each worshipper when he is 'lost in wonder, love, and praise'. This moment will not be the same for all. For one it may come in some word of the preacher's: for another it may occur during the reading of the lesson: to a third it may come in the singing of a hymn: to a fourth it may come in the silence. But for each it will give richer meaning to all the rest of the service so that they will feel it has been good to come up to the house of the Lord. Any service of public worship will have achieved its end—its divinely-appointed end—if those taking part in it can say with sincerity:

> *Lo, God is here! let us adore,*
> *And own how dreadful is this place!*
> *Let all within us feel His power,*
> *And silent bow before His face;*
> *Who know His power, His grace who prove,*
> *Serve Him with awe, with reverence love.*[7]

A satisfactory form and order for the public worship of God should give the proper place and proportion to each of the following elements: confession, thanksgiving, prayer, praise and adoration, silent waiting upon God, instruction and exhortation. In instruction and exhortation the congregation is in a sense passive; it has merely to listen, though with intelligence and attention, to the reading of the Scriptures or the sermon. The burden of activity is mainly thrown upon the minister. But in prayer and praise it is otherwise: the main activity should belong to the congregation. The function of the minister

[7] Tersteegen, translated by John Wesley (*M.H.B.*, No. 683).

PUBLIC WORSHIP IN FREE CHURCHES 17

and the object of the 'Order of Service' which he is using is to draw out its fullest extent the active participation of the congregation. This leads us to a detailed consideration of the various elements which make up the service.

PRAISE

In the worship of the Free Churches the hymns serve as a liturgy, as a response to the Gospel. As Bernard Manning puts it: 'Hymns are for the Dissenters what the liturgy, is to the Anglican. They are the framework, the setting, the conventional, the traditional part of divine service as we use it. They are the Dissenting Use. That is why we understand and love them as no one else does.'[8] The Free Churches have no set form of prayer: the only response that the people make is in the hymns they sing. The Word is read and proclaimed—the people respond in the hymn that follows. Prayer is offered—the people make the prayer their own in united song.

A collection of hymns is a means to an end, namely, the public worship of God. A hymn is made to be sung. On paper it is a dead form: given musical utterance it becomes alive. Unlike a work of literary art, the hymn-book therefore exists not in its own right, but merely as an instrument. 'Ideally a hymn should pass a double test—does it read well? and does it sing well? If it does one and not the other, it is not a good hymn, yet if it does both and lacks life it profits nothing.'[9]

What is a hymn? The classic definition is that by St. Augustine: 'It is a song with praise of God. If thou praisest God and singest not, thou utterest no hymn. If thou singest and praisest not God, thou utterest no hymn. A hymn, then, containeth these three things, song, praise

[8] *The Hymns of Wesley and Watts*, p. 133.
[9] F. J. Gillman, *The Evolution of the English Hymn*, pp. 27-8.

and that of God.'[10] This definition is inadequate because though it occurs in a commentary on the Psalms, it overlooks an element in hymnody in which the Psalms themselves are rich, that of petition. A hymn may contain prayer as well as praise, and in petition and intercession it may range widely in relating human needs and aspirations to divine provision for them. But one thing it may not do and that is to ignore God, for when it does that, it ceases to be a hymn.

A hymn is concerned with the expression of religious feeling of some kind. It should be cast in a metrical or at least a rhythmic form. To this extent it is the same as a religious poem. But the two need to be distinguished. A hymn is not necessarily a poem. As Bernard Manning has pointed out: 'It is incorrect to criticize hymns as if they were ordinary verses: to say of any hymn "it is not poetry" or "it is poor poetry" is to say nothing. A hymn like "Jesu, lover of my soul" may be poor religious poetry; but in face of the verdict of Christendom, only imbecility will declare it a poor hymn.'[11]

There are some words of John Newton written in the preface to the *Olney Hymns* in 1779 which may help in the differentiation between religious poetry and hymns. 'There is a style and manner suited to the composition of hymns which may be more successfully or at least more easily attained by a versifier than a poet. They should be Hymns, not Odes, if designed for public worship and for the use of plain people. Perspicacity, simplicity, and ease should be chiefly attended to: and the imagery and colouring of poetry, if admitted at all, should be indulged sparingly and with great judgement.' Newton's judgements were endorsed a century later by no less a person than Tennyson, who in a conversation with Dr. Warren, the President of Magdalen, remarked: 'A good hymn is

[10] Note on Psalm 72^{20}. [11] op. cit., p. 109.

the most difficult thing in the world to write. In a good hymn you have to be commonplace and poetical. The moment you cease to be commonplace and put in any expression at all out of the common, it ceases to be a hymn.'[12]

No hymn that has attained to world-wide fame and popularity bears the name of any poet of the first rank. Hymns may have the appeal that comes from the sincere expression of deeply-felt emotion, but the high imaginative flight that makes great poetry is not theirs and if it were the hymns would be less suited for their purpose. The ideal hymn is harmonious and dignified in its language but is at the same time free from all elaboration of thought and expression. A hymn such as 'O God, our help in ages past' contains no word or image that the simplest cannot understand. Yet the total effect of the hymn is to make it eminently suitable for use on the most solemn occasions.[13]

John Wesley in the Preface to *A Collection of Hymns for the Use of the People called Methodists*, issued in 1780, made these observations on the language of the hymns in the book.

'1. In these hymns there is no doggerel, no botches, nothing put in to patch up the rhyme, no feeble expletives.

'2. Here is nothing turgid or bombast on the one hand, or low and creeping on the other.

'3. Here are no cant expressions, no words without meaning. . . . We talk common sense, . . . both in verse and prose, and use no word but in a fixed . . . sense.

'4. Here are . . . both the purity, the strength, and the elegance of the English language, and, at the same time,

---

[12] Hallam, Lord Tennyson, *Tennyson: A Memoir*, Vol. II, p. 401.
[13] See *Hymnody, Past and Present*, C. S. Phillips, pp. 1-7.

the utmost simplicity and plainness, suited to every capacity.'[14]

It is important that not only the language and imagery of a hymn but also the sentiment should be suited to the ordinary worshipper. Nothing is worse than to put upon the lips of the people phrases that they do not and cannot mean. Many of the hymns used in worship are artificial. There is an air of unreality about them. They frequently express desires which no one shares or should wish to share. Some of them are marked by an excessive individuality which makes them unsuitable for general use in public worship.

The hymns the people sing have a vital effect on the formation of their spiritual character. Some words in the preface of the Supplement to the old *Primitive Methodist Hymnal* are worth quoting in this connexion: 'The value of a hymn in Christian worship is not determined exclusively or even mainly by its literary qualities. It is rather in its power to stir and express the feelings: to brace and stimulate the will: to kindle the pure flame of devotion: to bring the spirit of men into communion with God: to bind the worshippers in a unity that cancels all minor distinctions and gives them a sense of that vaster fellowship with the Church militant and triumphant.' In the Free Churches, where there is no prayer book as an aid to devotion, the hymn exercises an incalculable influence upon religious thought and feeling. As Evelyn Underhill expresses it: 'In the hymns, worship receives all the enhancement which music and poetry can give, and the peculiar effect of rhythmic corporate utterance in producing corporate feeling and enhancing individual sensibility is brought to the help of souls and the service of God. For the hymn enchants as well as informs: and here lies both its value and its danger.'[15]

[14] *Wesley's Works*, Vol. XIV, p. 353.   [15] *Worship*, p. 104.

Hymns, like the liturgies and the Scripture, are part of the accumulated heritage of the faithful. As they are read or sung, they serve as a reminder of past ages of the Church's life and bear witness to a fundamental unity among all Christians. A good hymn is one of the best means of impressing on men's minds the vital truths of the Christian faith. Paul spoke of the use of psalms and hymns and spiritual songs in the Early Church for 'teaching and admonishing one another'. John Wesley says in the Preface to his hymn-book already quoted: 'It is large enough to contain all the important truths of our most holy religion, whether speculative or practical; yea, to illustrate them all, and to prove them both by Scripture and reason. . . . So that this book is, in effect, a little body of experimental and practical divinity.'

The majority of the Church-going public judge a hymn more by the tune to which it is set than by its words. For the ordinary man music has a wider range of expression than has language. Robert Bridges, the poet, speaking to the Church Music Society about hymns said that the enormous power of the tune to create a mood is 'the one invaluable thing of magnitude which overrules every other consideration'. It is certainly true that the hymn-tune is an influential factor in worship. If it has the spiritual power which so many claim for it, the leaders of the Churches cannot afford to be indifferent to the musical content of their hymnals. For good or ill, the fortunes of a hymn-book are largely determined by the popularity of its tunes.

What is there in the character of music which makes it receive such general use in public worship? One reason is the directness of the appeal that music makes to the feelings. Some writers have protested against what they regard as the over-emphasis which has been placed on the emotional appeal of music. Dr. Farmer, for example, in lecturing to students training for the ministry, thinks it necessary to warn them of the dangers of music in worship. 'I confess', says he, 'I am a little afraid of music. It can so easily stimulate emotions far beyond any point to which real insight and genuine decision of will would ever take them. I suspect that in church many a man has mistaken the oscillation of his diaphragm in harmony with a ten-foot organ pipe or the quivering of his heart-strings to the melting sweetness of a boy's voice for a visitation of the Holy Spirit.'[16]

There is no doubt that there is a danger of music being used deliberately to stir people's feelings, and not to express the apprehension of God. Charles Wesley recognized this when he wrote:

> *Still let us on our guard be found,*
> *And watch against the power of sound,*
>   *With sacred jealousy;*
> *Lest haply sense should damp our zeal,*
> *And music's charms bewitch and steal*
>   *Our heart away from Thee.*[17]

Music not only impresses the feelings but likewise expresses them. It not only acts upon them from without but serves as an outlet to them from within. It is because the music is the expression of the composer's own feelings that it makes such a direct appeal to the feelings of the hearer. 'From the heart it has come,' wrote Beethoven of the *Kyrie* of his Mass in D, 'may it reach the heart again.' Music proves a valuable adjunct to Church worship because the worshipper is there, not as an inert listener but as an active participant, not merely to have his emotions played upon by the music, but to employ it to give utterance to the feeling that is welling up within him.

[16] *The Servant of the Word*, p. 76.
[17] *Poetical Works*, Vol. V, pp. 399-400.

Another reason for the use of music in religious worship is the affinity it holds with poetry.

> *Blest pair of sirens, pledges of Heaven's joy,*
> *Sphere-born harmonious sisters, Voice and Verse,*
> *Wed your divine sounds, and mixt power employ*
> *Dead things with inbreathed sense able to pierce.*[18]

The best of craftsman's art and music's measure is needed for the worship of God. Music and poetry should be, in John Wesley's phrase, 'the handmaids of piety'. The union of these two is a most happy one, for each can supply what the other lacks. The words of the hymn give definiteness to the feeling expressed by the music. Music alone is apt to be too emotional. Words alone are not emotional enough. 'Once recognize that music, so far from being a mere adjunct or decorative accompaniment to words, bears out and supplements their meaning with a subtle and persuasive language of its own, and the act of singing in worship acquires a new significance.'[19]

There is one other characteristic of music worthy of note which accounts for its use in worship, and that is its social nature. Church worship is essentially social in character. There is an individual and a social side to religion and due provision must be made for each. The aim of congregational singing should be to enable the people to experience a unity of heart and feeling one with another. Music will have amply justified its introduction into the worship of the sanctuary if it can claim to have strengthened the sense of fellowship which is the spirit of true religion.

The music of worship is part of the people's offering to God, and should therefore represent the best that they can give. In all Church music there is an underlying unity. Good hymn-tunes, whatever their origin, possess

---

[18] Milton, *At a Solemn Musick.*
[19] A. S. Gregory, *Praises with Understanding*, p. 202.

in common a certain stamp of worth and sincerity which transcends all their variations. It is surprising that, with so rich a treasury of incomparable music as has been accumulated in the course of the centuries, congregations should still continue to use music that is poor in quality and bad in taste.

A hymn sung fervently to the right tune is something different from either alone; it is a compound of the two, yet itself indivisible. This rapture of holy song is within everybody's reach. When Luther scoured Germany for suitable tunes he was not acting for specially musical people: the chorales were part of his revival. Early Methodist tunes were not in the least advanced or highbrow; their value lay in their expression of Methodist fervour. In the public expression of our common religious emotions music and words are alike indispensable. In their association with one another they afford a means of grace that is unique. Our thought of God and our service of Him is greatly influenced by the hymns we sing. In the same way music acts for good or ill upon religion. Only

If music and sweet poetry agree
As they must needs

is worship truly served.

The end to which all hymn-books are a means is the uplifting of hearts to God in corporate praise and prayer. In the light of this consideration of the place and purpose of hymns and tunes and their necessary union, how is the praise list for public worship to be drawn up? There are some leaders of worship who try to present one idea throughout the service, and hymns are chosen which will bear upon and illustrate that central idea. Prayers, lessons, praise, and sermon, are the repeated blows by which the one nail is driven securely home. From beginning to end of the service one thought and only one, is presented. There is something to be said for this. Ideas penetrate the minds of people more slowly than is sometimes imagined. The point of the sermon may be quite plain to the preacher because he has lived with it during the previous week and yet it may be missed by the congregation. It would seem a wise plan to prepare them by the hymns and Bible readings that they may the more easily grasp the lesson which the minister is trying to teach.

But there is something to be said against this practice. There is the obvious danger of monotony. When it is remembered that all classes and conditions and moods are to be found in the average congregation, it seems more useful not to make the service representative of one idea only, which necessarily limits its appeal and means that some needy soul may go empty away, but to seek to broaden the basis of the appeal. The most careful thought should be given, not only to the individual selections of what is to be sung, but to the congruity of what is chosen with its place in the order of service. There are three general principles which should be borne in mind in choosing the hymns.

The first is that a considered variety should be observed in the selection. It is a mistake, psychologically, to fit all the acts of praise into a single mould. There is a widespread predilection for what is known as 'hearty singing'. Nothing is more wearisome, and nothing tends to become more desolatingly unreal, than an unbroken succession of hymns that are sung, so to speak, with all the stops out. Always, in every congregation, there are people present who are undergoing heart-searching experiences, and to whom loud-voiced singing is the reverse of a natural or congenial expression; their need should be remembered. Even those who prefer singing of the hearty type will find the provision made for them more satisfying if, alternating with it, there are acts of a quieter order, penitential, meditative, devotional, such as accord with the need of those the lights of whose souls are burning low.

It is unwise to restrict the choice of hymns to those of an introspective type. It has been remarked as a weakness of Protestant worship that it tends to encourage individualism by making its acts egocentric. There is some justification for the criticism. Nothing is commoner than for people to estimate the value of a religious service by the subjective impression it has produced upon themselves. Introspective hymns that fix the mind on the emotions and concerns of the personal life should find only a subordinate place in the texture of public worship; the main themes should be objective, lifting the soul above its engrossing self-concern into adoring contemplation of the glory of God and His grace in Jesus Christ. The great hymns which express the glory of God in creation, providence, and redemption, and those which sing of the Incarnation, the Cross, Resurrection, and Glory of Christ, should be most frequently selected. The hymns which uplift and exalt are the strong, robust, manly hymns which the best Christian authors have given us, with dignity of thought, breadth of movement and worthy aspiration.

The second principle to be observed in the choice of the hymns is that of relevance: each act should be related to its place in the service and to the context of the other acts which form its neighbourhood. It often happens that the hymns chosen for a particular service wear a look of casualness, as if they followed a line of their own without relation to the general order of service, or as if they had been selected without any guiding principle at all. The choice of the hymns must not be casual or haphazard, or the service will be exposed to the risk of being spiritually a failure. The minister must not surrender his function of choice to anyone, since it is his responsibility alone to think of the spiritual proprieties at every point, of the relation of one part with another, and of the relation of all the parts to the whole. The hymns need to be carefully considered and their contents duly weighed, with a view to determining their possible influence on the entire worship.

The third principle that should be kept in mind is that of progression. There should be movement and change in the course of a service. It ought not to be a series of variations on a single theme. There is much to be said for restricting a sermon to the presentation and enforcement of a single idea; but when the one idea dominates the whole service, governing the choice of all the praise, the service is bound to suffer serious detriment. The service should not be allowed to become static in idea, but should move forward in a realizable progress, from point to point, in a clearly articulated order, advancing steadily as to a goal. The last hymn may be chosen to allow the congregation to express what it has been increasingly feeling while listening to the argument of the sermon, but 'appropriate praise' need go no farther, if the minister's desire be the good of the greatest number. For the rest, let the selection be as varied as possible, both in metre and subject-matter, that sorrow and joy, fear and hope, conflict and triumph, may all find speech for themselves in holy song.

PRAYERS

Once when a young minister asked Dr. Alexander Whyte whether he advised the preparation of prayers for the pulpit he received as his reply: 'Certainly I do, but public prayer is an unnatural act.'[20] Dr. Whyte felt prayer to be such an intimate, personal thing that he

[20] G. F. Barbour, *Life of Alexander Whyte*, p. 307.

shrank from the responsibility of shaping and uttering the prayers of others. There is a suggestive truth in his rather startling words. Private prayer is a natural and normal thing—the soul of a man pouring itself out to God. To pray before others and on their behalf, is by no means so simple, direct, and natural an exercise. But it is inevitable, since the Church is a fellowship. Whoever leads the worship of a congregation must seek to utter their united praise and petitions, gathering up into one all that is and all that ought to be in their hearts.

There are two diverse and contrasted ways in which the common prayer of the people may be offered—on the one hand by means of a prepared and authorized liturgy, and on the other hand by means of free prayer offered by the leader of the worship out of the fullness of his own heart. Both methods have much that can be said in their favour, and it will be of value if their respective merits and demerits are considered.

Consider first what may be said for and against a prescribed liturgy. The word itself comes direct from the Greek, where it meant a public office or duty discharged by a private citizen at his own expense. It came to be applied to Holy Communion and then to other set forms of public worship. This usage is derived from the Septuagint where the word is used to describe the service of the Jewish Temple.

In the earliest days of the Christian Church the Liturgy (as Holy Communion is still called in the Eastern Church) was made up mainly of extempore prayer. In particular was this the case with the central prayer of the service, the prayer of consecration. In course of time it became stereotyped by influence of habit. Once a satisfactory form of words is found, there is a natural tendency to use it again and again. This was one of the influences which gradually led to the rise of set forms of prayer.

Another reason for the development of a set liturgy was that common prayer which is designed to meet the needs of the congregation as a whole can only be expressed in general terms. Liturgical prayer is designed solely to bring before God the thoughts and desires of the whole congregation. The more particular thoughts and desires of individuals are excluded. It has a purifying and astringent effect upon the worshipper, for it lifts him out of his self-concern into the larger concerns of the Christian family. A liturgy is comprehensive, presenting a balanced and carefully considered expression of the common needs of man. Its materials have been drawn from the finest devotional literature of the past, and therefore its language is chaste and stately, with a charm of style which lingers in the memory. Streeter, speaking of the beauty of language and the devotional quality of the prayers in *The Book of Common Prayer* says: 'To expect a minister to produce, week by week, extemporary prayers which can rival these, is to demand that he shall be at once a spiritual and a literary genius.'[21]

Another factor which tells strongly in favour of a liturgy is the power of tradition. There is a peculiar inspiration which comes from the realization that the same form of words has been in use for centuries and that every Sunday thousands of Christians all over the world are using the same prayers. A liturgy may be regarded as the Church praying. It has something of that precious quality of Holy Scripture of which Newman says: 'It is far higher and wider than our need; and its language veils our feelings while it gives expression to them.'

Another value of a liturgy is that it affords a uniform means of worship and so serves to bind together all the members of a Church into one loyalty and to bring them into the larger fellowship of the Church universal.

[21] *Concerning Prayer*, p. 284.

A further advantage is that the people know what is coming next. They know exactly when to attune their minds to confession or thanksgiving or intercession. Moreover, they are saved from being dependent on the varying moods of the leader of the worship. The liturgy not only expresses what they feel, but it teaches them what they ought to feel.

One other value of a liturgy which deserves mention is its function in educating the worshipper in the historical basis of his faith. Here lies the importance of the Christian Year, with its recurrent reminders of the birth, manhood, temptations, death, and resurrection of Jesus as the framework of the Church's ordered devotion. 'The homely pieties of the Christian Year, directed as they are to the successive phases of God's redeeming action in history, point beyond themselves and witness to those profound spiritual realities which transcend history and yet give history its significance.'[22]

These arguments in favour of a liturgy are well summed up by a Presbyterian minister, Dr. Wallace Williamson: 'The obvious advantage to the worshippers of knowing beforehand what prayers are to be offered: the greater facility a liturgy affords for unanimity in worship: the continuity of the service through the living ages of the Church, a practical exposition of the communion of the saints—the fact that the worshipper is not at the mercy of the individual minister: the general dignity and reverence of liturgical expression: the truly catholic spirit thus engendered: the certainty that no abiding want shall be left unexpressed: the security that the Church possesses that the worship of God shall be rendered in all fullness, that the evangelical verities shall not be ignored or sublimated, that the faith of Christ shall be continually presented in a form more likely to mould the life of the

[22] Evelyn Underhill, *Worship*, pp. 73-7.

worshipper than the formal and abstract statements of the theological confessions—these are the main considerations which justify the use of a fixed liturgical form.'[23]

On the other hand there are considerations which tell against the use of a prescribed form of public prayer. There is grave danger of a liturgy becoming cold and formal. It lacks warmth, particular application and personal appeal. It cannot express the intimate desires and the changing aspirations of the ordinary man. It uses archaic language which tends to make the prayers remote. Familiarity can breed, if not contempt, at least indifference, and make the constant repetition of the same prayers mechanical and almost meaningless. The human mind rebels against monotony, and if the same service is used every Sunday many of the congregation will become listless and inattentive. Streeter admits that if prayer is to be made a reality, especially to the less spiritually minded, the Church of England needs to allow greater opportunity than is afforded by the *Prayer Book* for prayers about current events and matters of personal and local interest. No liturgy is completely satisfactory. The Morning Prayer of the Church of England is a combination of ancient offices and the patchwork shows. It has its roots in the ordered services of the monasteries and assumes that the main worship-occasion of the day— the Holy Communion—is over or is still to come.

A liturgy will always have the defects of its qualities. To be confined and restricted to a liturgy is to be hampered, for there is such a thing as the naturalness of prayer. There are prayers that are too perfect in their form and expression to be perfect as prayers offered to God. There is much force in the contention of Dr. James Black that a liturgy is more welcomed by the minister than by the

[23] *Ideals of the Ministry*, pp. 77-8.

people. 'Without any doubt', he says, 'its historical origin lies among the clergy. A form of prayer is an untold relief to the ministrant, for it saves him from a burden of worrying responsibilities, and most of all it saves him from himself.'[24]

What may be said for and against free prayer? The peculiar genius of the Protestant religion—the free and joyous spirit inspired by the doctrine of forgiveness—naturally seeks an opportunity for spontaneous expression. There are times when the minister would feel his spirit restrained and imprisoned if he were confined either to a printed liturgy or to words which he himself had written out for the occasion. The occasion itself will often suggest thoughts which no previous study would give. As we have seen, the growth of liturgies was a comparatively late development of the Church. Free prayer is an apostolic practice. It is natural speech and as such it has a power all its own. Its manner is that in which a devout Christian would talk to his Lord in private. It gives to the service a freshness and spontaneity which are impossible if the same form of words is used every Sunday. It is capable of reaching great heights and of deeply moving the worshippers. It allows for a tenderness of heart and a nearness to God that are not possible under any set form. It can be adjusted to the sudden needs of the nation, the Church, or the individual. Free prayer must continue to be used because of its elasticity. We need elasticity in order that we may be particular. Free prayer is rightly cherished in the Free Churches as one of Christ's most precious gifts of the Spirit to His Church. It is a prerogative and privilege we never can forgo.

The Free Churches are tied to no liturgy. There are no prayers which must be said, and no rubrics which have to be obeyed. Thus there is possible a directness, a freedom,

[24] *The Mystery of Preaching*, p. 229.

a particular appropriateness to occasions and seasons such as the Church of England can never possess. The worship of the Church is permanently impoverished where the untrammelled expression of a praying and Spirit-guided community is not allowed. The Free Churches in retaining the spontaneous expression of the common needs of the people have been preserving something of real value in worship.

But it must be admitted that free prayer, like a liturgy, suffers from the defects of its qualities. If the chief danger of a liturgy is formalism, the chief danger of free prayer is slovenliness. Dr. J. H. Jowett rightly says: 'There is nothing mightier than the utterance of spontaneous prayer when it is born in the depths of the soul. But there is nothing more dreadfully unimpressive than extemporary prayer which leaps about on the surface of things, a disorderly dance of empty words going we know not whither.'[25]

It is this disorderliness which makes it so difficult for the pew to keep up with the pulpit and in any real way to join in the prayer. Even when the prayer itself and the minister leave little to be desired, extempore prayer suffers from the great drawback that it demands considerable agility on the part of the congregation to follow a prayer which it has never heard before, because it does not know what is coming next.

The extemporary type of service makes a great demand on the personality and powers of the minister. It is too dependent on his moods, his failings, his culture, and his self-preparation. The prayers which are unprepared may err alike in what they include and in what they omit. Their language is often lacking in dignity and reverence and by its want of reserve it may wound the more sensitive worshippers. The prayers are often too long, which is a mistake from a psychological standpoint, for to most

[25] *The Preacher, His Life and Work*, pp. 154-5.

people intense concentration is difficult and can only be sustained for a short time.

Many Free Churchmen imagine that extempore prayer is confined to prayer that is conceived at the same moment as it is offered. They would regard a minister's preparation of his petitions in advance as a quenching of the Spirit. Prayer which is unpremeditated and spontaneous has a power all its own, if it is inspired by the Holy Spirit, but there are grave objections to regarding it as the only legitimate form of prayer. When the minister's prayers are wholly extempore there is an unnecessary poverty in the Church's worship. Spurgeon advised his students never to prepare a prayer and yet always to be preparing for their prayers. By this he meant that the minister should never prepare his words in advance but that he should constantly be steeping himself in the great language of devotion, pre-eminently the Bible, so that when the time came for public prayer, words suitable and worthy would come naturally to his lips.[26] If the minister does not prepare his prayers in any way, he will fall into a rut, and will use the same phrases continually, so that his people will be left with something like a liturgy with none of the mitigations of the great liturgies.

The minister's task is not merely or primarily to express the petitions that may be in his heart, but so to lead in prayer that his words kindle in the congregation the spirit of prayer. When he reads the Bible or preaches his sermon, he is acting as a prophet, but apart from these two duties, he acts during the rest of the service as a priest, speaking to God for the people. Dean Sperry rightly attributes most of the infelicities of free worship to the failure of the minister to realize that in the conduct of a service he fills two offices, not one. 'Free prayer', he says, 'tends to take on an informational nature or to become an

[26] *Lectures to My Students*, First Series, p. 70.

exercise in self-analysis. The poverty of the pastoral prayer reflects the concentration of the minister on his prophetic office, to the neglect of his priestly office.'[27]

The difficulty with most non-liturgical worship is that the author's 'hands and feet' are too much in evidence. Only a real artist or a saint can save the free service from those idiosyncrasies which tend to reduce it to a public display of private devotion. What gives reality to worship is a certain impersonality on the part of the one who officiates. The minister who leads in prayer is not an individual praying for himself, but is the voice of the people. The forms and words should be as transparent as a good clean window. A good window simply lets people see out and lets the light into the room where they are.

A liturgy is safe for it will never sink so low as free prayer, but it may never rise so high. The privilege of the Free Churches is that in their services they may combine the merits of both liturgical and free prayer. By making a judicious selection of the best prayers and forms of the universal Church with the principle of free prayer fully preserved, they may yet evolve a type of worship that may surpass any of the prescribed services of all the churches. The choice is not between a service which is confined to a liturgy and a service which has no liturgy. The issue is between more liturgy or less, good liturgy or bad. William Arthur, a distinguished Methodist minister of the last century in his once famous book, *The Tongue of Fire*, said: 'He who will never use a form in public prayer casts away the wisdom of the past. He who will use only forms casts away the hope of utterance to be given by the Spirit at present, and even shuts up the future in the stiff bonds of the past. To object to use forms is narrowness. To doom a Christian temple to be a place wherein a

[27] *Reality in Worship*, p. 307.

simple and impromptu prayer may never rise to Heaven is superstition.'[28]

Many think that the time has come when the Free Churches should give some place to forms of prayer, while always allowing an opportunity in every service for free prayer. There are three reasons why this change seems desirable: 1. There may be forced free prayer, when neither the mood nor the impulse nor the language of free prayer is present; 2. People have become more sensitive to the use of words, and prayers offered in public require careful expression in simple yet memorable words; 3. In free prayer there is no opportunity for audible response from the listeners and so the congregation is excluded from anything but silent participation except during the hymns.

There is much prejudice in Free Church congregations against 'read prayers' as being the opposite of 'praying in the spirit'. Dr. G. S. Stewart says that 'one of the most curious heresies infesting the Church is that the Spirit of God is hindered by watchful thought and only works through improvisation, that when a pen or a book is used prayer becomes "man-made" and dead'.[29] A man can hardly be too well prepared for leading the worship of God's people, provided that he leaves himself free to follow any leading of the Spirit that may come to him in the course of the service.

John Owen's principle is a sound one. He says: 'That only is a form of prayer unto any which he himself useth as a form; for its nature depends on its use.' The Free Churches are at liberty to adopt any forms that may be found helpful, provided that they are suitable to the occasion and in harmony with evangelical theology. Extempore prayer may become a form, a superstition, and a bondage.

The way to avoid this is to weave together prayer and

[28] op. cit., p. 21.   [29] *The Lower Levels of Prayer*, p. 120.

Bible-reading. God speaks to men through the Bible: they make response in appropriate prayer. Prayer divorced from the Bible is apt to become thin and unsatisfying. It is the Bible which sets the standard for man in the language of prayer, and where there is no such devotional model, extempore prayer often tends to be loose and undignified in its expression. Many simple and uncultured people have possessed a remarkable power in prayer. They read little but their Bibles, but when they prayed they fell back, as by an instinct, on the mother-tongue of their spiritual life—the noble speech of the English Bible. They knew nothing of literary style, but their prayers might have been printed as examples of chaste, restrained, and yet impassioned utterances of devotion.

Isaac Watts in his *Guide to Prayer* says: 'The Spirit of God will often bless the use of his own language, and I am persuaded that this is one way whereby the Spirit helps our infirmities and becomes a Spirit of supplication in us, by suggesting to us particular passages of Scripture, that are useful to furnish us both with matter and expression in prayer. It would be of excellent use to improve us in the gift of prayer, if in our daily reading of the Word of God we did observe what expressions were suited to the several parts of this duty—adoration, confession, petition, or thanksgiving—and let them be wrought into our addresses to God that day. Nay, if we did but remember one verse every day, and fix it into our hearts by frequent meditation and work it into our prayers morning and evening, it would in time grow up into a treasure of divine language, fit to address our Maker upon all occurrences of life.'[30]

No doubt these words apply more to private prayers, but they do apply to public prayers also. It is possible that a wise use of Scripture in the prayers of the congregation

[30] *Works of Isaac Watts*, Vol. III, p. 142.

might give us something that none of our present-day liturgical experiments have provided. In so far as words can mediate God, there are none like the words of Scripture. It is not for their verbal music that they are needed, though that has its appeal, but for the quality of the faith that inspired them.

In all public worship worthy of the name there are certain great notes which must be struck, and they will be most effective if they are struck in order. In the past it was the general rule in the Free Churches for the central devotional features of the service to be 'the long prayer' as it was called, in which was combined confession, thanksgiving, petition, and intercession. Mark Rutherford, in his *Autobiography* recalling the Sundays of his childhood, when he attended the services of the Bunyan Meeting-House in Bedford, says: 'The long prayer was a terrible hypocrisy, and it was a sore tax on the preacher to get through it. Anything more totally unlike the model recommended to us in the New Testament cannot be well imagined. It generally began with a confession that we were all sinners, but no individual sins were ever confessed, and then ensued a kind of dialogue with God, very much resembling the speeches which in later years I have heard in the House of Commons from the movers and seconders of addresses to the Crown at the opening of Parliament. In all the religion of that day nothing was falser than the long prayer. Direct appeal to God can only be justified when it is passionate. To come maundering into His presence when we have nothing particular to say is an insult, upon which we would never presume if we had a petition to present to any earthly personage.'[31]

Whether the long prayer deserves all the harsh things Mark Rutherford said about it or not, the sooner it is abolished the better. The prayers of the Bible, with very

[31] op. cit., p. 6.

few exceptions, are all short. If a service is to be conducted in such a way that all can take part in it to the utmost of their capacity, its guiding principle should be 'one thing at a time'. Confession, thanksgiving, petition, and intercession should not be combined in one long prayer, but should be divided from one another by the other and less exacting elements in the service, such as the hymns and readings from Scripture. Whenever in the course of prayer the congregation is asked to pass from one subject to another the change ought not to be sudden or unexpected. The minister knows beforehand what is to be the next subject of prayer, but the mind of the congregation needs notice of the change, and time to adjust itself.[32]

If free prayer is to be congregational worship, the worshippers must know the aim and movement of the prayer so as to be able to follow it. When Dr. Johnson, as reported by Boswell, makes the remark, 'Sir, the Presbyterians have no public worship; they have no form of prayer in which they know they are to join. They go to hear a man pray and are to judge whether they will join with him', he passes the criticism of an unsympathetic hearer. But the remark has value in this, that it points to the peril of free prayer that is not framed in the movement of a liturgy or shaped to the purpose of common worship. For public worship some formal character is essential. It is difficult for a congregation to pray with the spirit and the understanding in an improvised prayer because its attention is concentrated on the word spoken rather than on God. To allow the common mind to find in the prayer that is offered the expression of its own need in relationship to God, careful construction and preparation are essential.

At the outset of a service it is well to sound the call to worship. Much depends for the value of a whole service

[32] See *Concerning Prayer*, Streeter, p. 287.

upon how it begins. After the recitation of Scripture sentences which confront the soul with the reality of God, there naturally follows a prayer of Invocation, leading on to an act of Adoration. The note of wonder and of praise sounds first. The next prayer will be that of Confession, for after contemplating the glory of God we cannot but feel our utter unworthiness. Confession with absolution precedes thanksgiving so that the soul confessed and pardoned may praise with joy.

It is but a short step from the assurance of the forgiveness of our sins to Petition. The prayer of petition is the primitive prayer, but it is the abiding prayer. The petitionary element in prayer always makes for directness and simplicity. God has everything to give and we have everything to receive. Then follows Thanksgiving, the general thanksgiving for God's mercy and goodness and the special thanksgiving for particular things and happenings.

The last of the great notes to be sounded is that of Intercession. To be allowed to pray for others is one of the greatest privileges granted by God to His children. God makes a place for our prayers in what He pleases to do. It is a great act of Christian fellowship. It cannot be done too well. It deserves to be orderly, all-inclusive, and informed throughout with a Christ-like compassion.

The Free Churches need to experiment in the use of silence. There are two points at which its value is plain, at the beginning of the service, that in quietness the worshippers may find out what is the soul's sincere desire, and after the sermon. St. Augustine prayed: 'O Lord, who canst teach Thy faithful people without the din of words, teach us.' In ordinary worship something is always going on, somebody is always talking. Men need to learn that it is not only in seeking and doing, but in a wise passiveness that the soul is fed, that they must be still that they may know. 'He that truly possesseth the word of Jesus', said Ignatius, 'is able to hearken unto His silence.'

The ideal to which the Free Churches will tend to move more and more will be some form of worship in which liturgical, free, and silent prayer will all, in varying degrees, have their place. In this way, Anglicans with their matchless liturgy; Congregationalists, Presbyterians, and Methodists, with their greater freedom and spontaneity; and Quakers, with their great gift of silence, will all contribute to the enrichment of our common worship. Over a hundred years ago this ideal was expressed in a letter written by Baron Bunsen to Dr. Arnold of Rugby in 1834. 'I claim liberty for extempore prayer; liberty for silent prayer, and liberty for altering the liturgy. As long as the world stands there will be people who prefer a liturgy like yours; others who prefer extempore prayer: others, free selections from fixed prayers; but all reasonable men would allow such a form to be best, to be really catholic, which would unite all, assigning to each mode its fittest place.'

THE LESSONS

The practice of reading Scripture was taken over by the Church directly from the Synagogue service, and was an essential part of the Liturgy of the Catechumens, and it has ever since been regarded as an indispensable part of Christian worship. In the absence of any wide circulation of copies of Scripture it was at first the principal if not the only way by which the knowledge of God's Word could be conveyed to the people.

At first the number of lessons and the amount read were not fixed; and when these were determined there was great variety in the number of lessons. 'The Apostolic Constitution' has five and there is evidence of this extended use in the Eastern liturgies and in the Roman Mass. Eventually the number became three.[33] With the Reformation, a cardinal principle of which was that all worship is founded on the Word of God, it was natural that a new emphasis should be laid on this portion of the service.

In the opening moments of the service something has been done to 'break up the fallow ground'. The soil is to some extent prepared to receive the seed. No one who listens to the reading of the Bible with an attentive mind and a ready will can fail to receive a message from God. For the supreme value of the Bible is that through its varied writings God communicates Himself to man, and imparts His mind and will. 'The entrance of Thy word giveth light.' The Spirit searches the deep things of man and He uses the Word of God as His instrument.

The present tendency to reduce the reading of Scripture to one lesson is not only to be deplored but resisted. This imperils our position as evangelical and reformed Churches, and it lowers the tone of Divine Service by setting a false value on man's words to man. The Bible is a much misunderstood book, and there are many ways by which its meaning may be made clear and its message pressed home. A minister should regard the lessons as part of the opportunity God gives him of proclaiming the Word. He should select passages of vital importance and by his reading and, where necessary, explanation, will seek to make them the permanent possession of his people.

A passing comment is often necessary, but not a running commentary. 'And they read in the book, in the law of God, distinctly, and they gave the sense so that they understood the reading.'[34] All that is needed are a few words of preface setting forth the importance and meaning of the passage to be read, or putting it in its

---

[33] See D. H. Hislop, *Our Heritage in Public Worship*, p. 330.
[34] Nehemiah 8[8].

appropriate setting. Sometimes a sentence or two at the end may help to impress the message on the mind of the hearers. But the reading itself should not be interrupted by comment, for the Bible speaks most clearly when it is allowed to speak for itself. Dr. Denney said of his friend Struthers of Greenock: 'He never reads Scripture as if he had written it: he always reads it as if listening for a Voice.'

The reading of the lessons can be casual, unstudied and sometimes unintelligent. If it is the message of God and the source of our spiritual life, the reading of Scripture cannot be regarded too seriously or prepared for too carefully. As Dr. James Black says: 'It is more important to hear the Word than to hear words about it.'[35] As the majority of people nowadays do not read their Bibles at home, their attendance at Church is the one opportunity for the Bible to be made a living book for them.

There is a tendency in some Churches to depart from the custom of confining the lessons exclusively to the canon of Scripture. But no writings can have the authority and value of the Bible. Its message must be given a permanent and unique place in our service. Scripture stands alone, but there is a difficulty caused by the new attitude toward it in the light of modern criticism. Certain passages are unsuited to public worship because they are not in accord with the clearest and fullest revelation. There are other passages which, if they are interpreted, are of value, but without some explanation they may give rise to wrong views of God. The interpretation of Scripture is a vital need. For this purpose the occasional use of modern translations is of value. But as a general rule since public worship requires a special and liturgical speech to invoke the deepest associations, it is unwise to depart from the accepted and hallowed words. The

[35] *The Mystery of Preaching*, p. 216.

atmosphere of devotion may all too easily be disturbed by the use of commonplace language.

How are the lessons to be selected? The choice of such passages as suit the subject of the sermon is defended as a method which gives unity to the service, but this is at the expense of a greater unity, namely the unity of a complete service of Divine Worship, in which the varying needs and moods of the people find adequate expression. It is better to make the Word of God felt all through the service as its leading factor, than to make the preacher's subject the governing thought in the whole worship of each Sunday.

An American writer, Dr. Edwin H. Byington, in a book entitled *The Quest for Experience in Worship*, dealing with the way in which public worship may be made a memorable and enriching experience for all who share in it, says of the Scripture reading that there are three classes of Bible passages. '1, Those whose meaning is only apparent to the student working diligently with lexicon and commentary; 2, Those rewarding him who by himself reads slowly and carefully; 3, Those that are intelligible to people listening to a somewhat rapid public presentation.' The selections should as a rule, he argues, be taken from the third group. Many passages from the other two groups can be brought into the third by a few explanatory sentences—if it is historical, the statement might cover time, place, and situation; if it is an argument, let the preacher outline the drift of the discussion; if a letter, something of the writer and the recipients should be indicated.

It does not occur to most of the congregation that the minister has a special reason for choosing a particular passage, so it would be wise for him to take them into his confidence. There is spiritual value when two passages are read in conjunction to present a dramatic contrast, such as a prophecy and its fulfilment or the model man in the first Psalm and the model man of the Beatitudes. If the people realize the motive that has determined the choice of the lessons, they will feel a greater interest in the reading, and even the indifferent and listless will respond. The Scriptures are there to be read and interpreted to the congregation. The saving word concerning Christ is to be 'broken', as the Bread is broken and distributed at the Lord's Table, for the people are indeed at the same feast.

Once the independent value of the lessons is seen, it becomes obvious that the public reading of the Bible week by week should be guided by some principle and should follow an intelligible order. Where the preacher chooses his lessons to suit his sermon, the result will be that a number of favourite or familiar passages are repeated again and again, while the greater part of the Bible is neglected. If the congregation is to be given a view of Scripture in its completeness, then some kind of lectionary is called for, which will bring before them those portions of the Bible which are best fitted for public worship. In the *Book of Common Order* of the Church of Scotland, issued in 1940, there is a Scheme of Lessons which covers the Bible in two years and follows the course of the Christian Year. To follow such a course would restore the Bible to the place it ought to have in our services and bring before the minds of the people the fundamental doctrines of the Christian Faith.

'The lectionary required to meet the conditions which obtain in the Free Churches today is one which shall be so framed that even the "oncer" shall by means of it receive some impression of the continuity and majestic scope, the rich variety and the growing force, of Divine revelation as embodied in the Bible.'[36] The *Westminster Directory for the Public Worship of God* required that all the canonical books be read over in order, 'that the people

[36] J. Arnold Quail, 'Toward a Free Church Lectionary,' *Congregational Quarterly*, July 1930, Vol. VIII, p. 338.

may be better acquainted with the whole body of Scripture'. But there are grave disadvantages in this method. The directing principle in any selection should concern itself with the New Testament as the primary Scripture within the Christian Church and make use of the Old Testament as subsidiary thereto, either in the way of contrast or as that undeveloped revelation which is crowned in the writings of the new dispensation.

The people will profit by such a careful selection. They will come to realize that they are being led about the full circle of the Christian message. A preacher who allows such a lectionary to guide him will leave little untouched of all that he should deliver to his people in the course of the year, for their instruction and growth in grace. Besides that, he will find himself meeting, in a just and balanced fashion, the varying needs of his flock, from youth to age.

THE SERMON

Christianity began, not with a book, but with preaching. 'Jesus came preaching.' The very first thing laid down in the commission which the risen Lord left with His Church as its marching orders was: 'Go and preach.' The preaching of the Gospel received an essential and primary place in the Church's function from the beginning, and the age of preaching will only come to an end when our Lord's commission becomes obsolete. It is the spoken word— the foolishness of preaching—which from apostolic times has been the aggressive weapon of the Church. 'How shall they hear without a preacher?' There has never been a revival which has not had a preacher at its centre. The sermon belongs to the lifelong tradition of the Church.

'He who realizes the living place which preaching has

ever taken in the spiritual life of the Church will need no further assurance of its great importance. He will not fail to note that the preacher's message and the Church's spiritual condition have risen or fallen together. When life has gone out of the preacher, it is not long before it has gone out of the Church also. On the other hand, when there has been a revived message of life on the preacher's lips there comes as a consequence a revived condition in the Church itself. The connexion between the two things has been close, uniform, and constant.'[37]

Professor C. H. Dodd in *The Apostolic Preaching* has shown how the content of primitive preaching was of two distinct types. There was the preaching, or proclamation of the facts and events of God's action in Christ for the salvation of men (*kerygma*). Alongside of this there was also the exposition or teaching of an ethical ideal, the Christian life, personal and corporate (*didache*). Preaching contemplates two distinct results, for it is the Church's chief instrument for effecting the great ends for which the Church exists—self-propagation and self-edification, the conversion of the sinner and the building-up of the believer in his most holy faith.

Pastoral and evangelistic preaching, as these two types may be called, both date from the foundation of the Church. We naturally hear more in the first days of Christianity of missionary or evangelistic preaching than of pastoral or congregational preaching. In St. Luke's account of the midnight meeting in an upper room at Troas,[38] we have, for the first and only time in the New Testament the verb which afterwards furnished a name—Homily—for pastoral preaching, the address which was intended to give instruction in the things of the spiritual life.[39]

---

[37] John Brown, *Puritan Preaching in England*, p. 7.   [38] Acts 20^{11}.
[39] See J. O. Dykes, *The Christian Minister and his Duties*, pp. 185-7.

The division in practice between these two types of preaching is rarely a clean-cut one. A missionary who is addressing a purely heathen audience would confine himself to a proclamation of the Word, seeking the conversion of his hearers. If a congregation were composed of none but genuine Christians, the sermon would be of a purely pastoral kind. But every congregation is wider than the true Church, and includes hearers whose Christianity is but nominal. As a rule, therefore, preaching needs to be of a mixed character. But, primarily, preaching is not instruction or exhortation, but proclamation. It is the act by which the Church bears witness to the Word of God. That is why P. T. Forsyth describes preaching as the most distinctive institution of Christianity.[40]

The preacher is not in the pulpit to air his private opinions about anything, or to deliver his ideas about ethical, social, or religious questions, but to proclaim the faith once for all delivered to the saints. He is a herald, and an ambassador of Christ, and neither by his words nor by the spirit of his utterance must he veil the face of Christ or distort His message. This is the view of preaching which is characteristic of the Free Churches, while the Anglicans have tended to confine themselves to the idea of the homily. By placing the sermon after the benediction they have sought to distinguish it from the inspired liturgy which is often spoken of as the Divine Office. In some congregations in the Church of England it is by no means an unusual thing for many to rise and leave the Church at the point in the service when the minister mounts the pulpit to preach. They do not believe that the sermon is an integral part of worship, and with a good conscience leave the house of God as if the worship were ended.

In the Free Churches, on the other hand, there are

[40] See *Positive Preaching and the Modern Mind*, p. 3.

those whom we describe as sermon-tasters, who have only one test for determining the value of a service, and that is the quality of the sermon. Everything up to the sermon is spoken of and treated as 'the preliminaries'. When the critics leave the Church they do so with only one feeling, and that is praise or blame, appreciation or depreciation of the sermon.[41]

Both these so contrary attitudes are due to an entirely wrong conception of the sermon. To treat preaching and worship as if they were things to be set in contrast is a great mistake. It is true that as preacher the minister's attitude is distinguished from that in which he stands as leader of the devotional service. There he, along with his people, approaches God. In the pulpit he speaks to his people in the name of God. Yet, however sharp the distinction, so long as it is faithful to New Testament standards, preaching *is* worship. The preacher is a man under authority. It is the Word of God and not his own experience that he preaches. His commission is to proclaim the good news, and not merely to give good advice. The Anglican custom of prefacing the sermon by the formula 'In the name of the Father, and of the Son, and of the Holy Ghost', or by a short prayer for illumination, does remind both preacher and hearer that it is God's action, and not man's words from which the power comes. Again, at the conclusion of the sermon, the use of an ascription 'swathes the Word with prayer'. The action of beginning and ending the sermon by offering it to the glory of God exercises a healthy restraint on the mind of the preacher as to manner and matter. The manner will be such as befits a sacred occasion. The matter will be restricted to the sphere of religion.[42]

The sermon looked at as an act of worship is the

---

[41] See Frank Cairns, *The Prophet of the Heart*, pp. 50ff.
[42] See O. B. Milligan, *The Ministry of Worship*, p. 64.

highest view and the right view of its purpose. 'It is often said by those who worship in churches where preaching is at a discount: "We do not go to church to hear a sermon, but to worship God." No doubt there are sermons which justify such comments, but if the preacher's message is what it ought to be, if he is truly ministering the Word of God to his people, they are inept. He cannot deliver it without worshipping: and what, as Spurgeon said, can more truly be described as worship than hearing the Word of God as it demands to be heard—with faith, with reverence, with penitence, with personal application, with self-dedication, with abandonment of the soul to God our Saviour? . . . There ought to be nothing in the preaching that is inconsistent with worship, nothing that does not promote it in its purest and most spiritual forms.'[43]

At the Reformation, just at the point in the service where in the Roman Catholic form the Host was elevated, the Reformers put the sermon. The central place which had been taken by the Mass was claimed for the preaching of the Word in a context of prayer.

The Christian preacher stands in Christ's stead. The function of his sermon is nothing less and nothing else than to give to the people the words which Christ has given to him. While preaching is a preacher saying something, yet it is only distinctively preaching in so far as it is uttered and heard in the faith that it is God's activity, that through the medium of human words God is encountering human souls. So, as Dr. Farmer puts it: 'It is the sermon which can do more than anything else, under God, to keep the whole transaction of worship, so full of pitfalls and dangers, on the highest level of personal relationship. . . . From this angle, the wisdom of the Reformers appears in always associating the speaking

[43] Dr. James Denney, *The Church and the Kingdom*, pp. 18-20.

of the Word with other sacraments, and the Protestant habit, which is sometimes derided, of always having an address at every meeting, is seen to have sound sense behind it.'[44]

Modern man being psychologically minded rather than theologically minded cannot understand why the Reformers put the sermon in the centre of their worship. Good preaching, it is admitted, may have its place as an aid to worship, but in what sense can a human word addressed to man be itself worship of God? So Percy Dearmer says: 'To make the sermon the centre of worship is a psychological mistake as well as a theological blunder.'[45] It is all to the good that the sermon is no longer taken for granted. That preaching should be the central act of Christian worship is not a self-evident truth, but a startling paradox. Yet so long as we remain at the psychological point of view, we shall never understand the real nature of preaching and worship. When J. B. Pratt says that 'the sermon is Protestantism's greatest weapon in liberalizing and deepening religious thought and in directing the forces of the Christian community toward purity of private life and aggressive actions in the great struggle for social righteousness',[46] he leaves out the one thing needful, for he is describing the sermon only from the human side.

Preaching is not merely symbolic, it is sacramental. A symbol is the vehicle of an idea or an experience. It reminds us of what we already know. It can speak to us only in so far as it speaks from us. A sacrament is not a hint, but an event. The words of the sermon are not themselves the sacrament, but like the bread and the wine in Holy Communion are 'elements', symbols through which faith bears witness to the Word. Without symbols

---

[44] *The Servant of the Word*, p. 80. [45] *The Church at Prayer*, p. 138.
[46] *The Religious Consciousness*, p. 303.

faith would be dumb. But the Word that faith proclaims brings the very symbols into conformity with itself.

Unless the sacramental character of true preaching is realized, the real inwardness of Free Church worship will not be understood. Luther's view is that through the Word alive with the Spirit, 'The Lord is directly revealed to the heart of the worshippers in the Church: it is not ideas about Him nor memories of His life, but He Himself living and working in us.'[47] The Word spoken and the Word acted are both sacramental, and it is the Word which turns both the speech and the action into sacraments. The ordination of a Free Church minister is to the ministry of the Word and Sacraments. While the functions are distinct, they are not wholly separable. These two 'means of grace', as they are sometimes called, do not differ in what they convey but in their mode of conveyance.

It is man's response to the love of God in Christ as proclaimed in the preached word that makes the sermon sacramental. The real presence of Christ crucified is what makes preaching. It turns a speech into a sermon, and a sermon into Gospel. So John Wesley again and again in his *Journal* when describing his preaching says: 'I offered them Christ.' That is the evangelical note. Paul, Luther, Wesley, Spurgeon, and all the great preachers of the Church have offered Christ and the offer has been accepted. The idea of the sermon as being the mere exposition of the preacher's views is a modern development. It is a rationalistic way of looking at it, and reduces the sermon to the level of the lecture. Every true sermon is a sacramental act. If Christ instituted the Sacrament of Holy Communion, it is His Gospel which has set up the sermon. As Forsyth says: 'The sermon has always been regarded as an integral part of the service

[47] *Christian Worship*, ed. Nathanael Micklem, pp. 130f.

by a Protestantism which knew what it was about. It is the Word of the Gospel returning in confession to God who gave it. It is addressed to men indeed, but in truth it is offered to God.'[48]

This sacramental view of the preaching of the Word is a vital contribution of the Free Church tradition to the worship of the universal Church. Where the Free Churches are true to their traditional doctrine there is a sacramental character in the ordinary Sunday service which is not generally looked for in Matins or Evensong even when the sermon is added. It is noteworthy that the Churches which have exalted preaching have generally been indifferent to ritual, and that where ritual has been elaborated preaching has declined.

Preaching, then, stands at the focus of worship. If the sermon is not worshipful and is in contrast with and not a completion of the worship of prayer and praise, it has failed to be what Christian preaching ought to be. The service of prayer and praise should be dominated by the proclamation. 'We pray for many things, but above all that God will presently speak to us. We thank Him for all the blessings of this life, but chiefly for this, that we have heard His gospel of mercy and deliverance. We confess our sin and unworthiness, but only as we confess the grace and glory of His Son. The psychological unity of the service will be best secured by a more careful attention to the evangelical unity in which the sermon with its Biblical and contemporary witness to the Word is not just an item, but the organizing principle.'[49]

This view of preaching will mean that the people in the pew will be so actively receptive that the preacher will feel that his preaching is not his solitary act, but the collective act of the Christian community in the worship

---

[48] *Positive Preaching and the Modern Mind*, p. 97.
[49] Lovell Cocks, in *Expository Times*, Vol. XLIX, p. 264.

of God. Whatever preaching may do to exhort, direct, rebuke, edify, or inspire, it should do through the feelings awakened in the congregation by their acts of common worship. Only as it thus speaks to souls uplifted and purified can it exercise its true function and fulfil its God-appointed purpose. If the sermon is to be an act of worship it will need to be placed in a context of prayer, both the prayer of the preacher and the hearer. The sermon should be launched into an atmosphere made reverent and expectant by the spirit of prayer.

A pastor in seeking to fulfil his preaching office needs a system which shall enable him to adjust his message to the full round of his people's requirements, and so to declare the whole counsel of God. He is not left to his own resources in this matter, for there is available to him a complete scheme of the mysteries of the Christian religion, if he will but observe the Christian Year. It is both fitting and profitable for believers to dwell faithfully and regularly upon all the segments which together constitute the circle of the revelation of God centred in Christ. It is likewise fitting and profitable for the minister to guide his people in this way, for the observance of the Christian Year affords him generous help in his effort to preach in fullness the Gospel committed to him, and to accommodate it to the various needs of his flock, according to the different stages of their experience and growth.[50]

The scope of preaching must not be limited by a too narrow view of its function. One lesson from the past is that preaching has played many parts. It has been both teaching and exhortation. Sometime it has been the preparation for, and the supplement to, the worship offered in prayers and sacrament. Sometimes preaching is mainly instructive, being an exposition of Scripture or of some great doctrine. Sometimes preaching is a direct

[50] See A. Boyd Scott, *Preaching Week by Week*, pp. 79ff.

appeal to the will, to secure a verdict. A really live sermon has been described as 'a speech concluding with a motion', and though this does not cover every case, it must be admitted that there is something wrong with a preacher who does not frequently compel his hearers to face decisions. That is why Newman laid it down that 'definiteness is the life of preaching'. This quality is supremely necessary in what has been called 'the ministry of conquest', that is, the preaching which aims at conversion.

Preaching in its various forms is concerned with the Word of God as revealed to man, at times explaining it, which is expository or doctrinal preaching: at times pointing out its consequences in the life of men and nations, which is ethical preaching: at times creating the mood of worship, which may be called devotional preaching. The sermon has an importance, not as a substitute for symbolic worship but as the necessary accompaniment that enlightens the mind, warms the heart, and stirs the will to action. As Dr. Hislop puts it: 'If we are to build a worship catholic and free, it is largely through preaching that the new atmosphere must be created and the new spirit called into being. In this the sermon must be the servant of the spirit of worship. Amid these days, so fraught with peril and yet filled with promise, preaching never had a greater part to play in proclaiming the Faith nor a more urgent duty than to call forth the spirit of worship.'[51]

THE SACRAMENTS

God offers to men confirmation of the Gospel in the sacraments. The preaching of the Word makes its appeal through the ear: in the sacraments the Gospel is presented

[51] *Our Heritage in Public Worship*, p. 334.

by way of other senses also, and with a new vividness. Men do not receive from them anything different from what is made known in the Gospel, nor do the sacraments reveal a fuller redemption than that of which the Gospel tells. Christ, who in ordinary worship is presented through *words* in preaching, is presented in the sacraments through *actions*. The importance of the two is evident by the experience of the Church. As an old Scottish preacher, Robert Bruce, put it: 'The sacrament is appointed that we may get a better grip of Christ nor we get in the simple word. The sacraments are appointed that I might have Him mair fullie in my saul; that He might make the better residence in me.'[52]

Ordinary worship and sacramental worship are governed by the same conditions and aim at the same end. It is the same Gospel that is preached through the Word that is proclaimed through the sacraments. But while these two types of service should never be contrasted with one another, there is a clear distinction between them. What we do in ordinary worship is done in sacramental worship by the use of visible and tangible symbols, and their use proclaims that something has been done. The water has been sprinkled; the bread and wine given and received and thus it is proclaimed that a transaction has taken place. What we do in the sacraments is done in accordance with the instructions of our Lord. The words spoken are His words. It is He who stands at the font and takes the lambs of the flock in His arms and blesses them. It is He who stands at the table and takes the bread, blesses, breaks, and gives to men.

Baptism and the Lord's Supper are not mere adjuncts to preaching. In them the Word is made visible. The sacraments are never to be separated from the Word of God. The preaching of the Gospel is a direct preparation

[52] Quoted by R. S. Simpson, *Ideas in Corporate Worship*, p. 28.

for sacramental worship. The authority for the observance of the sacraments is the New Testament record of the practice of the Early Church. The belief that in the sacraments God in Christ bestows His gifts upon men carries with it the conviction that they must always be linked with the Scriptures which bear witness to His redeeming acts.

Every Christian communion which calls itself a Church attaches value to these two sacraments, and the essential features are the same in all branches of the Church. As Dr. Allen expresses it in his classic work, *Christian Institutions*: 'There are two features or institutions of Christianity which, more than any others, reveal its meaning and purpose—the sacraments of Baptism and the Lord's Supper. They stand forth as monuments against the Christian horizon at every point of time and space, the water standing for purification, the bread and wine for the sustenance of life: humanity purifying itself in order to sit at the banquet of the Eternal. Into these sacraments, in the successive eras of history, men have read their hopes and their fears, their aspirations, till they have become summaries of the Christian life.'[53]

It is profoundly significant that these two sacraments have been preserved through the centuries and that in them the thought of Christendom has found expression 'ere thought could wed itself to speech'. All the Churches which observe them would agree in regarding them as 'outward and visible signs of an inward and spiritual grace'. The difference between the Free Churches and the 'Catholic' Churches is to be found in the different answers given to the question, How is the invisible spiritual grace related to the visible sign? The 'Catholic' Churches teach that the sign or symbol conveys the grace to the recipient because of some quality in the sign apart

[53] op. cit., pp. 399-400.

from any spiritual activity on the part of the recipient. The Free Churches teach that the symbol demands for its effectiveness faith on the part of the recipient which enables him to lay hold on the offered grace.[54]

Washing with water, as a sign of spiritual purification, occupied a prominent place among the religious observances of the Jews.[55] When those who, under the influence of John the Baptist's preaching, repented were directed to be baptized as an outward sign of their new way of life, the act was one which commended itself to them as most appropriate. In like manner those who received the teaching of our Lord's disciples readily submitted to be baptized. What Christ did was not to introduce a new symbol or practice but to make what was well understood in its spiritual significance a permanent badge of membership in His Kingdom.

Three passages from the Gospels, if read together, will give a clear view of the meaning of Christian Baptism and the place it is intended to hold in the Christian Church—Mark 1[1-8], Matthew 28[18-20], Mark 10[13-16]. From these passages we learn:

1. That Baptism admits the person baptized into the membership of the visible Church.

2. That Baptism is an outward representation of the grace which is necessary to make the person baptized a member of the invisible Church. There is, as John the Baptist taught, a twofold baptism with water and with the Holy Spirit. The baptism with the Holy Spirit is the reality of which baptism with water is the outward sign.[56]

3. That Baptism with water is also a token of God's willingness to give the Holy Spirit to them that ask Him. It is intended to be the means of stimulating the faith of the parents and of Church members generally, in seeking

---

[54] See C. Anderson Scott, *The Church, its Worship and Sacraments*, pp. 76-9.
[55] Mark 7[3-4].
[56] Matthew 3[11].

for their baptized children that regenerating grace of the Spirit which Baptism proclaims and promises.

If the ordinance of Baptism is to be a real means of grace to the Church and glorifying to God, it is important that its administration should be marked by dignity, solemnity, and thoughtfulness. The indispensable acts which constitute the unchanging framework of the service are few and leave room for much variety in other parts.

1. The first of them is the reading of the words of institution.[57] It is often advisable to say a few words in explanation of this rite in view of the ignorance and indifference which prevail on the subject. A Free Church minister has on the one side to correct the tendency on the part of ill-instructed parents to regard the rite as an indispensable guarantee of their child's salvation, and on the other side to bring out its meaning and value to the children of believers as confirming to them the promised grace of the Gospel and marking the privileged place within the fellowship of the Church which is theirs by birth.[58]

2. The questions addressed to an adult candidate or to the parents of a child need to be known beforehand by those who have to make response, and therefore ought to be prescribed by authority and never departed from in form. They should always embrace two things: a profession of faith and a promise to discharge certain duties. The purpose of both in the case of an adult is obvious. It is on the ground of his personal profession of faith and promise of Christian obedience that he is received into the Church. Godparents in the Roman and Anglican communions make the same profession of faith and undertake the same vows to lead a godly life on behalf of the

---

[57] Matthew 28 [16-20].
[58] See J. O. Dykes, *The Christian Minister and His Duties*, p. 153.

child, implying that when he comes to years of understanding he will hold the faith and lead the life of a Christian. The unreality of such professions made in the name of an infant has always been felt to be a difficulty in the Catholic ritual. It is surmounted in the Free Churches by an emphasis on the present faith of the parents and their undertaking to instruct the child in the Christian faith and train him to be a disciple of Christ rather than on the child's own assumed future faith.

3. The administration of the rite. This may be by immersion, which is the most impressive and truly symbolic method, since it preserves the meaning of a death to the old life and rising with Christ to the new. But climatic conditions made it necessary to allow baptism by 'effusion' or 'aspersion', pouring or sprinkling the water on the body.

The symbolism of Baptism is far-reaching, for it is a reminder that men must die to live and that even the purest needs cleansing. It ought to be a marked Churchly occasion, at which the members of the Christian community promise to create an atmosphere in which the growth of the child into Christian faith and discipleship shall be as natural as the opening of flowers to the sun. Consequently baptism should, whenever possible, be a part of public worship, before the whole congregation who, by standing, assent to the vows which are laid upon them as well as upon the parents. The *Book of Common Order* adopted by the Church of Scotland in 1564, says: 'The sacraments are not ordained by God to be used in private corners as charms or sorceries, but left to the congregation and necessarily annexed to God's Word as sealed of the same, therefore the infant which is to be baptized shall be brought to the Church on the day appointed to common prayer and preaching.'

In the most recent *Book of Offices* authorized by the

Methodist Church, in the order for Baptism a question is directed to the Church following the questions asked of the parents. The minister says to the congregation: 'Dearly beloved, who are of the household of faith, through the high calling of God in Christ Jesus, and who are now in Christ's Name to receive this child, will you endeavour so to maintain here a fellowship of worship and service in the Church that he may grow up in the knowledge and love of God, and of His Son Jesus Christ our Lord?' To this the congregation reply: 'We will, God being our helper.'[59]

If the health of the mother or of the child is such as to make it dangerous for them to come to Church the minister should take an official of the Church with him to the home and encourage the parents to invite as many relatives who are members of the Church as may be convenient. 'At all costs, the pernicious and all too common idea that the sprinkling of water and the saying of a prescribed formula in themselves make a difference to the child should be banished and in its place must be put the idea of a reception of a little friend into the Society of which the Friend of all little children is the Head—a Society which is rededicating itself for the child's sake.'[60]

Low and unworthy views of the meaning and value of this sacrament are prevalent in the Free Churches. By some parents it is regarded as a family ceremony for the dedication or naming of their child. By others it is omitted altogether with no sense of loss. Against the indiscriminate christening of every child as a matter of course the Baptist Churches have been a standing protest. In Scotland, the law of the Presbyterian Church refusing the rite to all but the children of Church members has

[59] *The Shorter Book of Offices*, p. 23.
[60] J. R. P. Sclater, *The Public Worship of God*, p. 139.

tended to uphold a worthier conception of the sacrament.

There are those who hold the opinion that any infant should be baptized at the request of its parents, whether they have any association with the Church or not. Those who defend this practice maintain that every child belongs to God and has been redeemed by Christ, and that Baptism symbolizes this fact of redemption. In infant Baptism, according to this view, the parents recognize and accept the work of Christ and in His Name, present the child to God. This 'indiscriminate Baptism' is open to serious objection. It is often based merely on the desire to 'name' the child and is sometimes taken advantage of by those who are uneasy about their relationship to God and are held in the bondage of superstition.

There is no ground for holding that Baptism is necessary to salvation. Any Church may make a rule, as the Methodist Church does, that it will only receive baptized persons into its membership. The rite commends itself as one of high symbolic value as well as Scriptural authority. What is necessary to salvation is the faith in God through Christ, of which Baptism is the sign. Since this sacrament is the recognized way of publicly acknowledging faith in Christ and is attended by its own blessing, the neglect of its observance means a serious loss.

The more the true meaning of Baptism is realized and the more its relation to faith is emphasized, the more difficult does it become to justify infant baptism except on one ground. The practice of infant baptism is based on the recognition of the principle of the solidarity of the family. God deals with the individual in infancy through the family of which the child is a member and through the family to the child, on the ground of the parents' faith.

This, as Dr. Scott points out, is only an extension to the sphere of religion of the fact that everything of value to its life reaches an infant through the medium of the family.[61] The sacrament is a sign to the child of the privilege which is already his through being born in a Christian home, where he may grow up to be consciously a child of God. It is also a sign of God's purpose of grace toward the child as well as toward his parents. Just as by birth the child came into the world as the child of his parents, so by Baptism he is brought into the Church as a member of Christ.

If it be objected that Baptism can mean nothing to the child because he knows nothing of it, it might equally well be argued that the Cross means nothing to him because before he was born Christ died for his sins. Many of the things that are of most value to us are done for us, before we are able to appreciate their value. We were made Britons by an act we do not remember—our birth into a British home. Dr. Ryder Smith uses the symbol of a kiss as an illustration. 'Do a father or mother postpone its use till their little one is old enough to understand what it means and return it? They kiss him as soon as he is born, for the symbol expresses their own love for him. It is the token of the fellowship of the home. Baptism, rightly used, expresses and intensifies the fellowship of home with Christ. If the central thing in Christianity be fellowship with Christ, and if confession be but one of its consequences it seems to follow that Baptism, the symbol of the beginning of that fellowship, should fall when this fellowship begins, that is, in the first days of life.'[62]

Baptism is the first act in the economy of the Christian Faith. It is the first sign and symbol of God's boundless love for the soul of man. It is what God does for us through the sacrament and not what we do that is of prime importance. It is Christ who is taking the little child into His arms. It is into His body that this new branch is

---

[61] See C. Anderson Scott, *The Church, its Worship and Sacraments*, p. 87.
[62] *The Sacramental Society*, p. 134.

engrafted. It is His presence that we represent by words and actions. As Dr. Micklem puts it: 'As the king succeeds to the throne on the death of his royal father, yet the Coronation service is the formal, solemn, ratification and conveyance of the sovereignty, so while the children of Christian parents are born into the covenant of grace, baptism is the formal ratification, the seal of the covenant, in respect of each particular child.'[63]

As a consequence of the Christian training and atmosphere in the home and the Church the expectation is that in due time the child, when he is come to years of discretion, will make his own the vows made for him at his baptism. Those who have been baptized may when they grow up repudiate their Christian birthright, but it is impossible altogether to escape the influences of childhood. There is nothing magical about Baptism. It does not work automatically. But it does represent the promise that we belong to Christ and that His saving grace and endless love are ours. It is said of Luther that in moments of temptation, when he was hard-pressed by the devil and was conscious of his own weakness, he would cry out: 'I have been baptized' (*baptizatus sum*). When he doubted his own strength he called to mind the promise and the power of Christ.

The Church should see that what is done in Baptism is completed in vital membership. An opportunity should be given in the Service for Reception into full communicant membership for an open profession of faith to be made, as a confirmation by the adult of what was done for him as a child.

It seems clear that, apart from a doubtful text or two, the New Testament always speaks of adult Baptism. This is only natural in the beginnings of a movement, as on the mission field today, since the converts would be adults,

[63] *The Creed of a Christian*, p. 131.

who would be baptized on their confession of faith. But it seems to many that the Church was guided aright when it passed to the practice of baptizing the children of Christian homes, whether this was done in New Testament times or not. There is no hint that infant baptism was looked upon as an innovation, nor is there any record of divergent opinions such as exist today within the Church, or the suggestion that only adults should be baptized until long after New Testament times. In this, as in all other practices about which there is no authoritative guidance in the teaching of Christ, the Church, under the direction of the Holy Spirit, was led to adopt a practice which is manifestly in line with the mind of our Lord.

P. T. Forsyth has pointed out that the two Baptisms, infant and adult, are psychologically different, although they have in common the main thing—the connexion with the Word and its blessings in a Church that is faithful to it. The one flows from experience and the other seals and commits to it. 'In adult Baptism regard is had to the subject's past experience of the Word; in infant Baptism to a future experience expected and provided for within the Church. In the one we are baptized ON faith, in the other UNTO faith; but both are justified by faith only.'[64]

Each form of Baptism would seem to be equally justified, and it would be well to accept the historic situation and make the question an open one in the Free Churches, allowing either practice at choice. Baptism is wrong, not when applied to children, but when separated from the other means of grace, and especially from the Word whose vehicle it is. The Church should not give Baptism unless there is prospect of Christian discipline and nurture within the home or the Christian Society. For apart from that, Baptism can so easily degenerate into a magical rite instead of a saving grace.

[64] *The Church and the Sacraments*, pp. 201ff.

When we pass from the consideration of Baptism to that of the other Gospel Sacrament, we are at once aware of a greater diversity of opinion, even among the Free Churches. There are those who believe that the elements, the bread and the wine, 'contain grace'. Many would say, in the words of the Savoy Declaration, that 'worthy receivers outwardly partaking of the visible elements of this sacrament do then also inwardly, by faith, really and indeed, yet not carnally and corporally, but spiritually, receive and feed upon Christ crucified and all benefits of His death'.

Others hold the view commonly called Zwinglian: for these the service is primarily a memorial, bringing to mind the great sacrifice of Christ on the Cross. To many, the sacrament means little or nothing: they do not stay to it. If pressed for their reason, they would probably say that they see no use for and find no help in outward forms; they agree in the main with the Quakers. The majority of believers have no theory at all. They come because they find this to be the most solemn and moving experience in the Church's worship.[65]

The Free Church doctrine of the Lord's Supper is evangelical. To Free Churchmen the Lord's Supper is supremely a feast of fellowship. Hence for this service the alternative and beautiful title of Holy Communion is often used. In this solemn service fellowship is raised to its highest form alike in expression and activity.

It is fellowship between the soul and the Saviour. Christ Himself is present. 'His Presence makes the feast.' Whoever may conduct the service and distribute the bread and wine, he does it as the servant of Christ. Behind the human agent, there is the heavenly Form. It is the Lord Himself who presides, distributes the elements, and blesses the worshipping soul. In Zwingli's words he is

[65] See B. H. Streeter, *Concerning Prayer*, p. 323.

'*et hospes et epulum*'—both Host and banquet food, both Giver and gift. The Free Churches believe in the Real Presence of Christ, not in the elements but in the rite as a whole.

But this fellowship is more than personal: it unites us to our fellow-believers. 'We, being many are one bread, and one body: for we are all partakers of one bread.'[66] In the mystical teaching of Paul, we all eat of the one Bread which is Christ, and so we all become united in the one Body which is Christ. Hence this experience of unity produces a double conviction. First, there is a feeling of equality. There are no distinctions at the Lord's Table, for it raises all to the same level. In the second place, there is a feeling of oneness with all Christ's people. We have our place in the same Body of Christ to which the apostles and evangelists, the martyrs and confessors, the saints and prophets of every age have belonged. In the sacrament we are specially conscious of this kinship, because we are taking part in a sacred rite which links us directly to the Early Church, and has been universally observed by the faithful ever since.

This fellowship takes a still wider sweep. It embraces not only the Church militant here on earth, but the Church triumphant in Heaven. As Charles Wesley reminds us:

> *. . . all the servants of our King,*
> *In earth and heaven, are one.*
> *One family we dwell in Him,*
> *One Church, above, beneath.*[67]

So at the Lord's Table there is a vivid realization of the communion of the saints. 'Therefore with angels, and archangels, and with all the company of heaven, we laud

---

[66] 1 Corinthians 10^{17}.
[67] *Methodist Hymn Book*, No. 824.

and magnify Thy glorious name, evermore praising Thee.'

The Free Church teaching about the sacrament is simple, spiritual, and scriptural. It is simple because it is easy to understand. The broken bread and the outpoured wine are symbols of the broken Body and outpoured Blood of the Saviour. They are a reminder that He suffered and died on our behalf. But the bread and wine are not merely symbols: if we take them in faith, Christ uses them to impart His living Presence to our souls. 'The Body and Blood of Christ are verily and indeed taken by the faithful in the Lord's Supper.' The simplicity of this teaching has much to commend it. It does not shroud the sacrament in mystery. It escapes the charge of magic.[68]

This teaching is spiritual because its emphasis is upon inner relationships. The Free Church belief does not demand a celebrant who has been endowed with special virtue which enables him alone to make a valid sacrament. For a true sacrament all that is needed is a devout lover of our Lord, properly appointed to this office by the recognized authorities of the Church; properly appointed because while celebrating he represents the priesthood of all believers, and also in the interests of decency and order. Let such a one administer with a pure intention and the Lord will use his service for the conveyance of blessing.

This teaching is scriptural, not merely because it accords with the written word, but because it harmonizes with the scriptural method of embodying and conveying truth. In the Bible we find certain rites and ceremonies devised to bring God and man together. Christ took hold of one of these when He instituted the sacrament. He adapted an ancient rite to a holier purpose—the Jewish Passover became a Christian ordinance. He broke bread

[68] T. W. Coleman, *The Free Church Sacrament and Catholic Ideals*, pp. 13-15.

and said: 'This is my body'; He gave the disciples a cup and said: 'This is my blood of the new covenant.' Here is a symbol to be repeated, and by its repetition to become the means whereby the presence of Christ with His Church is realized and the benefits of His redemption are appropriated. As Professor C. H. Dodd has put it: 'In the Eucharist the Church perpetually reconstitutes the crisis in which the Kingdom of God came in history. At each Eucharist we are there—we are in the night in which He was betrayed, at Golgotha, before the empty tomb on Easter Day, and in the upper room before He appeared; and we are at the moment of His coming, with angels and archangels, and all the company of heaven in the twinkling of an eye at the last trump.'[69]

Thus we may say that in this eschatological sacrament 'past, present, and future are indissolubly united'. This is well expressed in an ancient definition of the sacrament by St. Thomas Aquinas which was repeated by the Puritan divine William Ames: 'The sacrament is a sign commemorative of the Passion of Christ, demonstrative of Divine Grace, and prophetic of Future Glory.' It is worth considering what this means.

The sacrament is, in the first instance, a commemoration. It has a backward look directing the thoughts of men to the infinite sacrifice once offered for the sins of the world, according to the word of our Lord at its institution: 'This do in remembrance of Me.' The Holy Communion is a witness to an historical fact, namely that once in human history God in Christ gave Himself for man's salvation. It pleads before God that 'full, perfect, and sufficient sacrifice, oblation and satisfaction for the sins of the whole world' which Christ made upon the Cross, thus turning the minds of the people to the merits of Christ.

[69] *The Apostolic Preaching*, pp. 234-5.

With solemn faith we offer up,
And spread before Thy glorious eyes,
That only ground of all our hope,
That precious, bleeding sacrifice,
Which brings Thy grace on sinners down,
And perfects all our souls in one.[70]

This is the foundation of the Evangelical doctrine of Holy Communion. We look back to something done in the past. In faith and prayer we commemorate Christ's sacrifice before God. John Owen, a century before Wesley, bore witness to this same truth. In this ordinance of the Lord's Supper, 'Christ makes a double representation of Himself. He presents Himself unto God. He presents Himself unto us . . . as one that hath actually accomplished the great work, not as one that can do these things, nor as one that will do these things, but as one that hath actually done this, actually made peace for us, actually blotted out our sins and purchased eternal redemption for us.'[71]

But more than a commemoration of the past is needed. The hearts of men crave a present Saviour, not merely one who lived and died long ago, but one who is alive for evermore, and with us, according to His promise. The sacrament meets this need forasmuch as it is 'demonstrative of Divine Grace'. It has not merely a backward look but an upward look. It brings men into immediate fellowship with the living Saviour.

The Lamb as crucified afresh
Is here held out to men;
The tokens of His blood and flesh
Are on this table seen.

The Lord's Table is the place where above all others the soul is moved to penitence and also to thanksgiving.

[70] *Methodist Hymn Book*, No. 723, Charles Wesley.
[71] *A Book of Personal Religion*, ed. Nathanael Micklem, p. 122.

Here and now we are enabled to make the offering of ourselves, to unite the sacrifice of 'our souls and bodies' with the 'full, perfect, and sufficient sacrifice' of Christ.[72]

The sacrament has not only a backward look, and an upward look, but a forward look. It is 'prophetic of Future Glory'. Here is the significance of the words of our Lord in the upper room. 'I will not drink henceforth of this fruit of the vine until that day when I drink it new with you in my Father's kingdom.'[73] That earthly table was a symbol and prophecy of the Heavenly Banquet, the glad feast of homecoming. The Holy Communion is not only concerned with an act done in the past for man's salvation, it is not only the means whereby in the present believers may partake of the 'innumerable benefits' which come from that act, but it is also a service in which the Church looks on into the future. 'As often as ye eat this bread and drink the cup, ye proclaim the Lord's death, till He come.'[74]

> *And thus that dark betrayal night*
> *With the last advent we unite,*
> *By one blest chain of loving rite,*
>   *Until He come.*[75]

The sacrament of the Lord's Supper is the most moving presentation of the whole Gospel of God for men which the Church possesses. The union that is formed between Christ and the believer in that service calls forth the highest kind of worship and the most fruitful response. We are bound to ask how frequently this chief ordinance of the Church ought to be celebrated. There can be no doubt that the primitive Church observed it every Sunday and this practice was maintained for the first fifteen

---

[72] *Prayer and Worship*, Sermon by W. F. Flemington, p. 81.
[73] Matthew 26^{29}.   [74] 1 Corinthians 11^{26}.
[75] *Methodist Hymn Book*, No. 773, George Rawson.

hundred years of the Church's life. Calvin favoured a weekly celebration and was only prevented from putting it into practice at Geneva by the opposition of the civil powers. Richard Baxter held a like view. In Scotland a rubric in the *Book of Common Order* shows that it was John Knox's intention that the sacrament should be observed monthly. But after a time a yearly celebration (which Calvin had called 'an invention of the devil') became prevalent. During the troubles of the Commonwealth the Lord's Supper is said to have been neglected for years in many parishes of the three Kingdoms.[76]

In some lands, notably in Scotland, many Presbyterians have gone to an extreme of infrequency, and observe the sacrament only twice a year. The reason for this is not that they undervalue the ordinance, but that they regard it with a veneration so exalted that, as Dr. Dykes points out, it almost borders on superstition.[77] As the supreme act expressing communion with Christ it was accounted a season of rare devotion to be prepared for with care. There is something to be said for rarity of celebration: great public ceremonials intended to express the common life of a society lose their vitality and power if they come at frequent intervals. Infrequency tends to bring out a large proportion of the members. In the old days in Scotland the Communion was preceded by fast days and services of preparation, and it was followed by a service of thanksgiving. This had the effect of making the sacrament a high and exceptional feast.

Dr. Sclater, himself a Presbyterian, considers the modern method of having Communion as often as once a month to be the worst of compromises between the Anglican custom of having the Table always ready and the Presbyterian custom of having it spread twice a year.

[76] See O. B. Milligan, *The Ministry of Worship*, pp. 98-9.
[77] *The Christian Minister and His Duties*, p. 159.

He says: 'It is not nearly frequent enough to meet individual needs, and is too frequent to keep impressiveness as a Church festival.'[78] The solution he offers is to have great Churchly Communions very rarely and at them to use the Presbyterian mode, in which the whole of the membership remains seated as if round a common table and is served by elders, thus suggesting the communal aspect of the Supper: and to have very frequent Communions in which the individual aspect is emphasized, either after morning or evening service, and at these to use the Anglican mode, whereby each communicant advances to the Table and receives the elements separately.

It is a characteristic rule of the Reformed Church that the Communion service is preceded by a sermon: in Scotland this was called the Action sermon, a phrase which is more Latin than English, as it refers to the *actio gratiarum* —the giving of thanks—for on such an occasion the preacher could have only one theme—the recognition of a favour passing measure. This prepared the communicants for the feast to follow. The result has been that the sacrament follows the usual congregational worship on the Lord's Day. The reason is to be found in the Reformed doctrine of the sacraments as means of grace, ancillary to the Word of God. Luther said: 'The Word and the Word alone is the vehicle of grace.' Thus the sacraments do not add anything to the message of the Word about Christ's finished work; they do but movingly illustrate it. The Lord's Supper and the preached word are alike 'the Monstrance' of the evangel, which is prior to both.

The Reformed Churches set aside the name 'altar' and the ideas associated with it, and in its place put the scriptural name 'table' and the ideas suggested by the words 'Lord's Supper'. By bringing the communion table into the centre of the Church they made the worshippers

[78] *The Public Worship of God*, p. 164.

gather round the Supper table instead of standing before an altar. If sometimes the pulpit is behind the table, the suggestion is not that it is more important than the table, but rather that it is not a place which has any right of its own from which anything may be said, but a place where the preacher deals with one subject, the gospel and fellowship of which the table is a symbol.

'A Reformed service often in its architectural and liturgical arrangements, and always in spirit, refuses to separate word and sacrament. An ideal Free Church service today will incorporate in any arrangement of sacraments, hymns, prayers, and preaching, the Catholic emphasis on fact, the Lutheran note of personal experience, and the note of personal appeal characteristic of modern evangelism.'[79] The sacrament preaches the Word when the pulpit is silent. The preacher can only deal with aspects of the Word, subject as he is to the limitations of time. But the symbols and the liturgies of the Eucharist teach the gospel of redemption all the time. It is a constant witness to Christ incarnate, Christ present, Christ redeeming. It is the perpetual proclamation of the Lord's death till He come. Men in the pulpit can preach anything and often do, but the Holy Communion cannot help proclaiming the Gospel of the Word.

Sacramental worship is not without its perils, but it is none the less the precious heritage of Evangelical Christianity. Sacerdotalism is the danger, but it is a peril well understood and is easily avoided when met by the true priesthood of the whole Church, which must function if it is to be preserved. P. T. Forsyth rightly claims that the answer to Sacerdotalism is Sacramentalism.[80]

The Holy Communion is the most objective of all our services. The congregation not only sees something done,

[79] *Expository Times*, Vol. LIII, pp. 136-7.
[80] ibid., Vol. XLIX, p. 394.

PUBLIC WORSHIP IN FREE CHURCHES 75

they join in doing something and have a personal share in what is being done. They receive and they give. Both the external accompaniments and the spiritual content of the service combine to bring before us as nowhere else the fact of our Lord's presence.

The essential elements of a Communion service are few. There is first the reading of the words of Institution from one of our four sources, usually from the earliest, in the First Epistle to the Corinthians. Then there is the Prayer of Consecration. This requires to group together in a single act and in befitting language four distinct states of devotion. Their natural order would seem to be as follows: 1. An acknowledgement of our unworthiness; 2. Thanksgiving for God's love in our redemption through Christ; 3. A profession of our trust in His atoning death for the remission of our sins, which we are about to commemorate; 4. An invocation of the Holy Spirit to bless the elements, consecrating them into a means of grace to our souls.[81]

In the course of this prayer the minister should take the bread and break it in the sight of the people and likewise lift the cup and present it as he speaks the words concerning it. These 'manual acts' as they are called, are of value as part of the dramatic symbolism of the service, following as they do the recorded actions of our Lord Himself. The Presbyterians have always preserved this tradition, but in the other Free Churches this practice has fallen into disuse.

The third essential feature of the Communion service is the distribution of the elements. In all the Free Churches except the Methodist this is done by elders or deacons. The general Methodist practice is for the minister to distribute the bread and wine to the communicants who come to receive them kneeling at the communion rail. In most places the common cup has been displaced by

[81] See Dykes, op. cit., pp. 165-6.

individual cups. It would be unfortunate if this practice should lead to the loss of the feeling of community which the common cup symbolized. It was to set forth unity that the Early Church celebrated as it did. 'The cup of blessing which we bless, is it not a communion of the blood of Christ?'[82] By the sharing of the one cup the unity of the brotherhood was expressed and strengthened.[83]

The custom of the individual cups must be judged of by the hygienic reasons adduced in its favour. At first sight it appears to miss the sense of unity conveyed by common participation. After all, however, no large congregation which partakes simultaneously ever does drink literally out of only one cup: and it can make no difference in principle whether the wine be distributed into four or a hundred separate vessels. But, however sound this reasoning may be in logic, the sentiment of partaking in common is seriously wounded when no two drink out of the same vessel. It is difficult to find a satisfactory solution to this problem. One thing at least is evident, that there must be a chalice on the Communion table, for without it the symbolism is all wrong, and the minister is unable to perform the manual acts.

The fourth indispensable element in the service is the act of thanksgiving and self-dedication which should follow the receiving of the bread and wine. Without such an act the service would be incomplete. Everything has led up to and now everything is to be crowned by an act of self-giving. In full and glad surrender the communicants offer themselves afresh to their Lord.

Throughout the whole of this solemn service of worship it is essential to preserve the utmost possible order, silence, and freedom from distraction. Ministers cannot be too careful that every detail should be arranged beforehand,

---

[82] 1 Corinthians 10^{16}.
[83] See E. R. Micklem, *Our Approach To God*, p. 263-6.

so that there may be the right atmosphere in the Church. When Communion follows the ordinary morning or evening service, that service should be shorter than usual, and should be made an ante-communion service, in which the minds of the people are prepared for the sacred feast. Communicants should not be invited to enter into the most solemn service of the Church otherwise than in an attitude of eager expectation. The spirit of the service is one of tender emotion. It is the heart and not the intellect which is here called into play. One would give much to have the opportunity of sharing in a celebration of the Lord's Supper when all who were together might realize something of that wonderful sense of an approaching Presence which Walter Pater describes in his *Marius the Epicurean* as the characteristic feature of the Eucharist in the second century:

'"*Adoramus te Christe, quia per crucem tuam redemisti mundus*"—they cry together. So deep is the emotion that at moments it seems as if some there present apprehend that prayer prevails, that the very object of this pathetic crying himself draws near. From the first there had been the sense, an increasing assurance, of one coming: actually with them now, according to the oft-repeated petition: "*Dominus vobiscum*". Some at least were quite sure of it; and the confidence of this remnant fired the hearts, and gave meaning to the bold, ecstatic worship, of all the rest.'[84]

[84] op. cit., Vol. II, p. 138.

Part Two

The Methodist Church—A Detailed Survey of its Worship

METHODIST WORSHIP: ITS ORIGIN AND DEVELOPMENT

IT HAS been rightly said that it is impossible to understand Wesley if he is thought of only as a flaming evangelist and as a man with a rich personal experience. Behind that experience and that love of souls, there stands his institutional religion. He never failed to urge its importance on his followers. The first rule, for example, of the 'Bands', the little companies of devout persons, limited to four in number, who met together to confess their sins one to another, was that each member 'be at Church and at the Lord's Table every week'.

A Belgian Franciscan priest, Dr. Maximin Piette, has written an elaborate study of Methodism which was called in its original French edition *La Réaction Wesleyenne dans l'Evolution Protestante*.[1] There are senses in which the reaction of John Wesley on Protestantism was a Catholic reaction. He emphasized the social character of religion by means of corporate spiritual life which found expression in the class-meetings, band-meetings, and other organizations which he introduced. He laid great stress upon the sacraments as embodying the experience of the whole Church of Christ. As Dr. Rattenbury says: 'In some ways the Protestant Reformation in its natural protest against the ecclesiastical abuses of the sixteenth century may have

[1] English edition under title: *John Wesley in the Evolution of Protestantism*.

gone too far in the direction of individualism, and a Wesley was needed to restore the balance. His religious method, both inside and outside of Methodism, has shaped modern Protestantism more definitely than any other thing.'[2]

Wesley remained always a faithful son and priest of the Church of England. His friend, Alexander Knox, bears witness to this when he writes: 'In his prevalent tastes and likings as an individual he was a Church of England man of the highest tone; not only did he value and love that pure spirit of faith and piety which the Church of England inherits from Catholic antiquity; but even in the more circumstantial part there was not a service or a ceremony, a gesture or a habit for which he had not an unfeigned predilection. He was not only free from every Puritanical leaning, but the aversion to those early enemies of the Established Church which he had imbibed in his youth, though repressed and counteracted, was by no means wholly subdued even in the last stages of his life.'[3]

He said to his people at the Conference in Bristol in 1768: 'To leave the Church is to leave me,'[4] and yet at the same time he so organized the Methodists that everyone knew that sooner or later their links with the Church of England would be broken. He was convinced that God had raised him up to do a great work of evangelism. 'Church or no Church,' he said to the Bishop of London, 'we must save souls.' When he was asked whether this or that thing might not lead to schism, he replied that he could not refuse to do good now, because something might happen in the future.

It has been assumed by some writers on Methodism that the evangelical conversion which John Wesley

[2] *Wesley's Legacy to the World*, p. 167.
[3] Quoted in *The Conversion of the Wesleys*, p. 207.
[4] Luke Tyerman, *Life and Times of Wesley*, Vol. III, p. 23.

experienced on 24th May, 1738, at the meeting-house in Aldersgate Street, when his 'heart was strangely warmed', changed his High Church views and made him a liberal Churchman, if not a Dissenter at heart. This is not supported by the evidence. He kept his conversion experience alive by the free expression he gave to it. His devotional life was fed by constant Communion, by participation in public worship in parish Churches, though rarely by the sermons he heard there (to judge by many of the comments in his *Journal*), but also by his own elaborate method of private devotion, and by his fellowship with the members of the Methodist Societies, his helpers and his friends, many of whom were Anglican clergymen.

Wesley was well aware that great emotional experiences have their dangers. He delighted to use his brother's hymns to arouse the enthusiasm of his people, but at the same time he sought to establish them on the solid foundation of Christian tradition and discipline. So he reminded them that their services were supplementary to the services of the Established Church and he made it plain that he did not wish them to be substituted for the liturgical and sacramental worship and the ordered discipline of the Catholic Church.[5]

In many parishes, Methodists were excluded from the Holy Table. In others, they were unwilling to receive the elements at the hands of men whom they believed to be unworthy of their high calling. Some of Wesley's preachers insisted that they should have the right to administer the sacraments as well as preach. In the Conference of 1744 the question, 'Do we separate from the Church?' was answered: 'We do not. We hold communion therewith for conscience' sake, by constantly

[5] See Umphrey Lee, *John Wesley and Modern Religion*, pp. 242ff; and J. E. Rattenbury, *The Conversion of the Wesleys*, pp. 206ff.

attending both the word preached and the sacraments administered therein.' But Wesley was already being forced to face the possibility that after his death, the Methodists might secede from the Church. By 1755 the situation was tense, for the preachers were pressing Wesley hard, and in September of that year he wrote to the Reverend Samuel Walker that some of the arguments put forth he could not answer, and that his decision to remain within the Church rested on no good premises. But he insisted that the essence of the Church to him was not in her orders and laws but in her doctrines and worship.[6]

Wesley did not intend that his Methodist Societies should be taken for a Church. When Troeltsch wrote that Methodism 'belonged essentially to the sect-type and not to the Church-type, in spite of its earnest desire to remain inside the Established Church',[7] he was thinking of the Methodist Societies and not of Wesley's own ideal for them. It is difficult to avoid the conclusion that Wesley wished them to be societies within the Church. He came to prefer the simplicity of Methodist meetings to the drawling of clerks and the unedifying sermons of unawakened clergymen. In a letter to a correspondent in Truro in 1757 Wesley made a comparison between the worship of the Established Church and that of the Methodist Societies. He begins: 'The longer I am absent from London, and the more I attend the service of the Church in other places, the more I am convinced of the unspeakable advantage which the Methodists enjoy: I mean even with regard to public worship, particularly on the Lord's Day. The church where they assemble is not gay or splendid, . . . nor sordid or dirty; . . . but plain as well as clean. The persons who assemble there are not

---

[6] See *Letters of John Wesley*, Vol. III, pp 144-7.
[7] *The Social Teaching of the Christian Church*, Vol. II, p. 721.

a gay, giddy crowd, who come chiefly to see and be seen; nor a company of goodly, formal, outside Christians, whose religion lies in a dull round of duties; but a people most of whom do, and the rest earnestly seek to, worship God in spirit and in truth. Accordingly they do not spend their time there in bowing and curtseying, or in staring about them, but in looking upward and looking inward, in hearkening to the voice of God, and pouring out their hearts before Him. It is also no small advantage that the person who reads prayers, though not always the same, yet is always one . . . whose life is no reproach to his profession, and one who performs that solemn part of divine service, not in a careless, hurrying, slovenly manner, but seriously and slowly, as becomes him who is transacting so high an affair between God and man.[8]

Yet, in spite of this and other letters which might be quoted to show that Wesley had not the least intention of giving up the Methodist Societies, and that he considered their religious services superior to the general services of the Church of England, he insisted that Methodist services were purposely designed not to be worship, as that term is understood technically. The Methodist service was worship, but not such as superseded the Church Service. At the Conference in Leeds in 1766 Wesley entered very fully into the great question that was agitating his followers—that of separation from the Church of England. To the question 'Are we Dissenters?' the answer was given: 'We are irregular: 1. By calling sinners to repentance in all places of God's dominion. 2. By frequently using extemporary prayer. Yet we are not Dissenters in the only sense which our law acknowledges, namely, persons who believe it is sinful to attend the service of the Church; for we attend it at all opportunities.'

[8] See *Letters of John Wesley*, Vol. III, pp. 226-7.

Wesley goes on to deal with an objector who might say: 'Our own service is public worship.' He agrees that in a sense it is, but that it presupposes public prayer, like the sermons at the university. 'If it were designed to be instead of Church service, it would be essentially defective; for it seldom has the four grand parts of public prayer; deprecation, petition, intercession, and thanksgiving.' He ends by advising all the Methodists in England and Ireland who have been brought up in the Church, constantly to attend the service of the Church, at least every Sunday.[9]

This is a remarkable utterance. It shows clearly that Wesley regarded his own evangelistic and fellowship services not as substitutes for, but as supplements to, ordered public worship, and this no doubt accounts for his advice to his American preachers when he founded the Methodist Church in their country, and also for his counsel to preachers in English preaching-houses in 1786: 'We advise everyone who preaches in Church hours to read the Psalms and the Lessons with part of the Church prayers; because we apprehend, this will endear the Church service to our brethren, who probably would be prejudiced against it, if they heard none but extemporary prayers.'[10]

Many Dissenters crowded into the Methodist Societies, and a host of men and women belonging to no Church at all came under Wesley's influence or were converted under his lay-preachers. At first he told the Dissenters that they must attend the services at their own chapels; the rest of the members were supposed to come to short services on Sundays held in their own preaching-houses out of Church hours and afterwards to attend the services in the parish Church. But in 1780 the problem had become

---

[9] See *Wesley's Works*, Vol. VIII, pp. 321-2.
[10] Luke Tyerman, *Life and Times of John Wesley*, Vol. III, p. 478.

complicated by the erection of many Methodist preaching-houses in different parts of the country. The attitude of the clergy and the unfriendliness of the mass of the Church people had kindled an irresistible desire to have places in which Methodists could worship in peace. In examining the *Large Minutes* of 1780 we find among the 'warnings' contained in them, that the preachers are directed to warn the people 'against calling our Society the Church; against calling our preachers ministers, our houses meeting-houses: Call them plain preaching-houses or chapels'.[11]

At the same time the Methodist Societies in America were clamouring for the sacraments and for men empowered to administer them. On 2nd September 1784 Wesley set apart Dr. Coke as Superintendent of the work in America, and then proceeded to ordain two of his preachers, Vasey and Whatcoat, to journey to America as elders. He sent a letter to the Methodists of America, in which after declaring his appointment of these men, he adds: 'And I have prepared a Liturgy little differing from that of the Church of England (I think, the best constituted national Church in the world), which I advise all the travelling preachers to use on the Lord's Day in all the congregations, reading the Litany only on Wednesdays and Fridays, and praying extempore on all other days. I also advise the elders to administer the Supper of the Lord, on every Lord's Day.'[12]

This Liturgy was entitled: '*The Sunday Service of the Methodists in the United States of America: With other Occasional Services*: London: Printed in the Year 1784.' In the Preface to the book Wesley writes: 'I believe there is no Liturgy in the world, either in ancient or modern language, which breathes more of a solid, scriptural,

---

[11] See John Simon, *John Wesley: The Last Phase*, pp. 159-60.
[12] *Letters of John Wesley*, Vol. VII, p. 239.

rational piety than the *Common Prayer* of the Church of England: and though the main of it was compiled considerably more than two hundred years ago, yet is the language of it not only pure, but strong and elegant in the highest degree. Little alteration is made in the following edition of it, except in the following instances:

'1. Most of the holy-days (so called) are omitted, as at present answering no valuable end.

'2. The service of the Lord's Day, the length of which has been often complained of, is considerably shortened.

'3. Some sentences in the offices of baptism, and for the burial of the dead, are omitted; and,

'4. Many Psalms left out, and many parts of others as being highly improper for the mouths of a Christian congregation.'[13]

At the Christmas Conference in 1784 held at Baltimore, at which the Methodist Episcopal Church came into being the *Sunday Service of the Methodists in the United States of America* was adopted for use in the new Church. The *Minutes* of the 1784 Conference were printed in Philadelphia in 1785, and were bound up with the *Sunday Service* and a *Collection of Psalms and Hymns*, both of which had been sent over in loose printed leaves by John Wesley. In 1786 a new edition of this whole book was printed in London. According to the historian, Robert Emory, this was the last edition of the *Sunday Service* printed for the use of the American Methodists. Subsequently the *Minutes* became known as *The Discipline*. The Articles of Religion, and the Forms for administering the sacraments, for marriage, burial, and ordination, became appended to *The Discipline* and later became known as the *Ritual* and the collection of Psalms and Hymns became the *Hymnal*. The *Sunday Service* proper was laid aside soon after its introduction and was not used again.

[13] *Wesley's Works*, Vol. XIV, p. 317.

Many factors contributed to the disuse of Wesley's Liturgy among the Methodists in America. The people, being mostly labourers and farmers, were not used to its elegant literary style. To many new Methodists it must have savoured of the old unpopular Established Church. To many American citizens it must have been reminiscent of a State Church. Doubtless the most important reason was that, worshipping in open fields and rude forest chapels, they felt liturgical worship to be not only incongruous but unnecessary and even harmful. At any rate, the *Sunday Service* was neglected and while it has never been officially abrogated, and while the chief *Occasional Services* were taken over into the *Ritual*, the forms of the *Sunday Service* were quickly laid aside and almost forgotten.

This edition of the *Prayer Book* for America was issued in 1786 (with slight changes) as *The Sunday Service of the Methodists in His Majesty's Dominions* and in 1788 as *The Sunday Service of the Methodists*, according to Tyerman. Green's *Wesley Bibliography* records the first edition published in 1786, a copy of which is in the Rylands Library, Manchester. Dr. Bett says that Wesley's revisions were such as an Evangelical dissenter would make today.[14] Dr. Rattenbury thinks that they are due to Wesley's passion for abridgement and his desire to get as much of his *Prayer Book* as he could in use in America, where the Puritan tradition was strong.[15] Proctor and Frere make no reference at all to Wesley's revision in *A New History of the Book of Common Prayer*, though they refer to alterations in the American *Prayer Book* from 1785 onward, which appear to have been influenced by the Methodist revision.

Throughout the book Wesley uses the word 'minister' instead of 'priest', except in the Communion service

[14] See *The Spirit of Methodism*, pp. 67-8.
[15] See *Proceedings of Wesley Historical Society*, Vol. XXIII, pp. 173-5.

where the word 'elder' is used. In the Public Baptism of Infants, Wesley dispenses with signing the child with the sign of the cross, and leaves out the sentence in the thanksgiving, that 'it hath pleased God to regenerate this infant with His Holy Spirit'. The Order of Confirmation is omitted, as is any reference to god-parents. Another omission is the Order for the Visitation of the Sick. In the marriage service Wesley left out the ring ceremony, and in the burial service the committal. In place of the three forms for the ordaining of 'deacons, priests, and bishops', he gives three for ordaining 'superintendents, elders, and deacons'. In every rubric that calls for a chant or anthem, the demand for singing was deleted. ('Then shall be said or sung' became with Wesley: 'Then shall be said.') Wesley also abridged the Thirty-nine Articles and reduced them to Twenty-five. He took out of the Article on Baptism all reference to any impartation of grace, and made it affirm that baptism is a sign of the Christian profession and 'a sign of regeneration or the new birth'.

Wesley omitted the words 'Holy Communion' from the title of the service, leaving only the words 'the Lord's Supper'. The Nicene Creed was omitted; there were several changes in the Offertory Sentences; the three long Exhortations were deleted; the phrase, 'the burden of them is intolerable', was left out of the General Confession; the Absolution was changed into a Prayer for Pardon. Wesley provided that the prayers following this should be said by minister and people standing, which served to break up the long succession of kneeling in the Anglican service. He retained the Proper Prefaces before the *Sanctus*, but appointed them only for the proper day, and not throughout an octave. The *Sanctus* was to be said, not sung. The Manual Acts were retained, but the direction to receive kneeling was omitted. Wesley specified the use of the entire Consecration Prayer when a second consecration was necessary. This was probably to get away from the idea, inherent in the structure of the Anglican Office, that it is the repetition of the words of Institution alone which consecrates. The second Thanksgiving Wesley omitted altogether. He specified the use of the first Thanksgiving, which is really the Prayer of Oblation from the Consecration prayer which had been deliberately dislocated and placed in this inappropriate place in the Second *Prayer Book* of Edward VI. Wesley introduced a place for extempore prayer before the Blessing, at the discretion of the Elder. The Blessing itself was changed by adding the optative 'May' at the beginning, making it more of a petition than a priestly benediction. The collects at the close of the English service were all omitted, as well as the final rubrics. Throughout the service Wesley substituted 'elder' for priest'.

A study of the Liturgy prepared by Wesley reveals that the changes in the old *Prayer Book* asked for by the early Puritans were largely met by Wesley. Like most ritualistic revision his was a paring away of matter which he judged to be either redundant or harmful. We have noted, in his preface to the work, Wesley's own admiration for *The Book of Common Prayer*, and the solid scriptural piety to be found there. In a letter from Dublin, on 20th June 1789, he writes concerning the *Sunday Service*: 'Dr. Coke made two or three little alterations in the *Prayer Book* without my knowledge. I took particular care throughout to alter nothing for altering's sake. In religion I am for as few innovations as possible.'[16]

In an interesting article in the *Wesley Historical Society Proceedings*, the Reverend Frederick Hunter claims that Wesley's revision was chiefly inspired by suggestions which were made by the Presbyterians at the Savoy

[16] Luke Tyerman, op. cit., Vol. III, p. 580.

Conference of 1661.[17] In a letter already quoted, written in 1755 to the Reverend Samuel Walker of Truro, Wesley said that some of his preachers felt that they ought to separate from the Established Church, for the following reasons:

'1. Though the Liturgy is, in general, possessed of rare excellence, "it is both absurd and sinful, to declare such an assent and consent, to any merely human composition", as is required to it.

'2. Though they did not "object to the use of forms", they durst "not confine themselves to them".

'3. Because they considered the decretals of the Church as "the very dregs of popery", and "many of the canons as grossly wicked as absurd. The spirit which they breathe is throughout popish and antichristian.'[18]

Wesley then makes this comment. 'Those ministers who truly feared God near an hundred years ago had undoubtedly much the same objection to the Liturgy which some . . . have now. And I myself so far allow the force of several of those objections that I should not dare to declare my assent and consent to that book in the terms prescribed. Indeed, they are so strong that I think they cannot safely be used with regard to any book but the Bible. Neither dare I confine myself wholly to forms of prayer, not even in the church. I use, indeed, all the forms; but I frequently add extemporary prayer either before or after sermon. In behalf of many of the Canons I can say little; of the Spiritual Courts nothing at all. I dare not, therefore, allow the authority of the former or the jurisdiction of the latter.'[19]

Mr. Hunter points out that this is practically a summary of Chapter 10 of Calamy's *Abridgement of Mr. Baxter's*

[17] *Sources of Wesley's Revision of the Prayer Book in 1784–8*, Vol. XXIII, pp. 123–33.
[18] Tyerman, op. cit., Vol. II, p. 208.
[19] *Letters of John Wesley*, Vol. III, p. 152.

History of His Life and Times, which Wesley in his *Journal* records himself as having read in April 1754. That chapter deals with 'The grounds of the Nonconformity of the Ministers who were ejected'. This confirms the belief that Wesley made his revision of the *Prayer Book* in 1784 with Calamy's book before him. It was in that book that Wesley familiarized himself with the position of the Presbyterians of the Restoration period in respect of the *Prayer Book*. 'His revisions were dictated by love of that "Baxterian" Church of England, which would have comprehended at least his Presbyterian and perhaps also his Congregational ancestors.'[20]

After Wesley's death two distinct parties arose within Methodism. The first consisted of leading laymen who retained a great deal of old-fashioned Episcopalian feeling and wished Methodism to be 'if not a pillar inside, at least a buttress outside the Church of the nation'. They preferred to receive the Lord's Supper at the hands of episcopally ordained clergymen, and so to keep up a connexion with the parish churches. The second consisted of preachers and a large body of the people who preferred to receive the elements at the hands of those whom they regarded as their spiritual guides and who shrank from approaching the parish altar where perhaps there would be a clergyman who did not command their respect. The contest between the two sections became strong and the feeling was increased by a suspicion in some quarters that a few preachers were aiming at the establishment of a Methodist hierarchy. But an amicable settlement of the dispute was made at the Conference of 1795, when a Plan of Pacification was drawn up, whereby the sacrament was not to be administered in any chapel unless a majority of the trustees and leaders allowed it.

[20] Hunter, op. cit., p. 133.

THE METHODIST CHURCH 91

But the division continued as we can see by a comparison of two speeches made in the Conference of 1834. Jabez Bunting said: 'When we gave our people the sacraments in our own chapels we publicly guarded against its being taken as a sign of separation: I hold in my hand a letter of Charles Wesley's in which he says: "All the difference between my brother and me is, my brother is first for the Methodists, then for the Church. I am first for the Church, and then for the Methodists." We are the best Methodists when we imitate the spirit of John Wesley. Dissent when we must, but be on friendly terms when we can.'

This speech provoked a retort by Dr. Beaumont: 'Mr. Wesley, like a strong and skilful rower, looked one way while every stroke of his oar took him in the opposite direction. He never resolved that he would go no farther from the Church. We must have room to breathe and move our arms. I do not like to be tacked on to the Established Church. Let us retain our ancient liberty.'[21]

Wesleyan Methodism stood in sympathy and temper of mind between the Church of England and the Free Churches. It could rightly claim to be one of the most comprehensive Churches. Its government united elements of New Testament episcopacy and features of Presbyterianism. Its ministry was neither autocratic nor servile. It had sufficient breadth and elasticity to combine the most aggressive evangelistic methods with the simple and reverent use of ancient forms of praise and prayers.

There prevailed among the leading ministers of the Wesleyan Church in the earlier part of the nineteenth century a love for the liturgical service of the Church of England, though some of them did not like Wesley's abridgement. When the Reverend Joseph Entwistle consulted Dr. Adam Clarke as to the introduction of an

[21] Benjamin Gregory, *Sidelights on the Conflicts of Methodism*, pp. 155-6, 161.

organ and the Liturgy into Brunswick Chapel, Liverpool, he received this reply. 'With respect to the introduction of the Liturgy of the Church of England—this book I reverence next to the Book of God. Next to the Bible it has been the depository of the pure religion of Christ; and had it not been laid up there, and established by Acts of Parliament, I fear that religion would, long ere this, have been driven to the wilderness. Most devoutly do I wish that, wherever we have service on the forenoon of the Lord's Day, we may have the prayers read. This service contains that form of sound words to which, in succeeding ages, an appeal may be successfully made for the establishment of the truth professed by preceding generations. Had it not been, under God, for this blessed book, the Liturgy of the English Church, I verily believe Methodism had never existed. I see plainly that, where we read these prayers, our congregations become better settled, better edified, and put farther out of the reach of false doctrine. Introduce the Church Service in God's name, not in any *abridgement*, but in the genuine original.'[22]

Dr. Jabez Bunting, the most influential minister in the counsels of the Church during the first half of the nineteenth century, believed in a mode of worship which united the advantages of a liturgy and of extempore prayer. One recommendation of a liturgy to him was the obligation it imposed on the congregation to join audibly in public worship, thus abolishing the idea that the minister sustained to them any priestly office and placing him and them in acts of prayer and praise on one common level before God. Dr. Bunting had been familiar from his earliest childhood with the Liturgy because his parents had taken him regularly every Sunday to a parish Church in Manchester. When he was in a London circuit in 1803, he wrote in his diary 'Sunday evening Oct. 2nd. I read

[22] T. B. Bunting, *Life of Dr. Bunting*, Vol. I, p. 386.

THE METHODIST CHURCH 93

prayers at Wapping this forenoon (making, I believe, but one blunder).' A footnote says that the reading of the morning Service was a novelty to him, for in Oldham and in Macclesfield, where he had previously ministered, the services at the chapel were still conducted as supplementary to those of the Church of England.[23]

In the last few months of his residence in the Liverpool circuit a new chapel was in course of erection and it was suggested that an organ be put in it and 'many persons wished to introduce not only an organ, but the use of the Sunday morning service of the Church of England. Both were innovations at Liverpool, though organs had been permitted in a few cases elsewhere, and though the reading of the service, either in full or in an abridged form, always sanctioned by Wesley when service was performed in our chapels in England during Church hours, was the subject of a strong recommendation by the Conference in one of the Articles of the Plan of Pacification. . . . Upon the subject of the Liturgy he [Bunting] laid claim to an absolute impartiality. When he first engaged in the ministry the novelty of reading the Morning Prayers was, for a while, somewhat distasteful to him; but practice overcame this reluctance, and his experience in Methodism ultimately made him a decided friend to the general use of them. He did "not consider the use of forms of prayer as in all cases unlawful", but he did "object to being confined to forms of prayer". . . . He thought that where a congregation could be induced to concur in a mode of worship which united the advantages of a liturgy and of extemporaneous address to God, the case of the people and the general purposes of worship would be better served than by an adherence to one of these plans only. When, therefore, the Liturgy was used in the earlier service of the sabbath, though not even

[23] ibid., Vol. I, pp. 27, 190.

then to the exclusion of free prayer', while extempore prayers only were adopted at later services, Bunting's views and wishes were fully met. He 'always and strongly discountenanced any attempt to enforce the use of' Morning Prayer upon Methodist congregations. 'When any large proportion of a congregation, deprived of what it considered a privilege, was eager to obtain it, it was his practice to recommend them to wait until the erection of some new chapel might enable them to gratify their desire, without introducing an innovation, and arousing the spirit of strife.'[24]

T. P. Bunting says that his father would not have been able to accept all in *The Book of Common Prayer*, and adds in a footnote: 'I do not think that he would have felt less hesitation if he had been required formally to profess his assent to all and everything contained in the *Service Book* published by John Wesley. He strongly condemned the abbreviation of the Psalms; and he repudiated, as utterly unscriptural, the principle on which it was vindicated. Like Adam Clarke, he always preferred to use *The Book of Common Prayer* rather than the abridgement of it. . . .'[25]

Robert Newton, another prominent Methodist minister of the same period, went to London West Circuit in 1812, his previous circuits having been in Scotland and the North of England. In most of the London chapels he found the Liturgy was in use in the Sunday morning service. 'At this period,' says his biographer, 'he contracted such a love for the Liturgy that in future life it afforded him a sincere satisfaction to be appointed to circuits where the people were accustomed to the use of it. The Liturgy recommended itself to his ear and taste by the rhythm of its periods and the force of its diction and to his heart by the evangelical sentiments which it

[24] ibid., pp. 381-5. [25] ibid., p. 138.

embodies and the spirit of pure and elevated devotion by which it is pervaded. The comprehensiveness of its petitions for all classes of the human race gave expression to the expansive charity of his sanctified heart and in the use of this "form of sacred words" he felt himself able to worship God in spirit and in truth.'[26]

Richard Watson, an eminent Methodist theologian of the nineteenth century devoted over eight pages of his *Theological Institutes* issued in 1826 to showing that the position of those who object to the use of a liturgy in public worship is illogical and contrary to scriptural teaching and Apostolic practice.[27] When the centenary of the founding of Methodism was observed in 1839, Thomas Jackson compiled a special commemorative volume by order of Conference. In the course of it he says: 'The incomparable Liturgy is regularly used in many of the chapels in England and in all the Mission chapels of the West Indies. Translations of it have been made by Wesleyan missionaries into various languages for the use of their congregations, especially in the East. It is always used in the Lord's Supper at home and abroad.'

During the last century Wesleyan Methodism, both in theory and in practice, united the two types of worship which divide Christendom—the liturgical and the non-liturgical. Many of its prominent ministers, whose work lay mainly in the large town chapels, in many of which the *Prayer Book* was used, showed a marked preference for it, as ensuring the dignity, and comprehensiveness of Divine Service. The stately service matched a stateliness of person and demeanour which was characteristic of the ministerial leaders of the nineteenth century. At the same time, in the thousands of village chapels which were built in the

[26] Thomas Jackson, *Life of Robert Newton*, p. 76.
[27] See Vol. III, pp. 259-67.

first half of that century, chapels which only saw a minister occasionally, the Liturgy was never used.

As time went on, and Methodism continued to expand, the simpler form of service came to predominate and the order of service in all branches of the Methodist Church, with a decreasing number of exceptions, conformed to the extempore type traditionally followed in the Free Churches. This was inevitable as a result of the divisions that arose within Methodism, leading to the founding of other Methodist bodies which were more democratic in outlook and had no ties with the Church of England. There are still a number of churches which belonged to the Wesleyan section of the now united Church which continue to use on Sunday mornings the Order for Morning Prayer as Wesley revised it, and in many parts of the mission field it is in general use. Missionaries feel it to be particularly valuable for small village congregations, themselves not well instructed, whose worship is usually led by a native catechist. The Liturgy sets a standard of worship that would be otherwise impossible to reach.

The bulk of Methodist congregations in this country, however, feel that the archaic, though stately and rhythmic, language of the Liturgy, is too remote from their common speech. They find it difficult to enter into prayers read from a book, and it does not come home to them that a free prayer listened to from a pulpit is often hard to follow. The feeling is so widespread against a liturgy that its use is fast dying out, except for the sacramental services and occasional offices, such as marriages and burials, for which the use of the *Book of Offices* is almost universal.

St. Stephen's Green Methodist Church in Dublin used to have its own *Prayer Book* with alternative services for each Sunday of the month. In 1916 the Reverend W. J. Tunbridge published a similar book which had been in use for some years in some of the Wesleyan Churches in India. It was called *Public Worship: A Book of Responsive Services*. In the preface the compiler says: 'The Protestant Churches of the British Empire have hitherto followed two systems. The services of the Established Church have been enriched with the liturgy of *The Book of Common Prayer*, which in spirit and phrasing is unsurpassed; but it lacks flexibility, and many of the most devout are conscious of its monotony. The Free Churches have enjoyed more freedom, and long experience has taught them the value of extempore prayer. Yet it must be acknowledged that their system is defective chiefly because the congregation is so largely passive except in the singing of the hymns. Some congregations of the Established Church desire greater liberty than they possess at present, and the members of the Free Churches are learning the value of ordered and responsive services. It would seem, therefore, that the ideal is to be found in a combination of the two methods.'

After the Union of the Methodist Churches in 1932 a Committee was appointed to prepare a series of responsive services for use in public worship, and of orders of service for Church festivals and other special occasions. This book, called *Divine Worship*, was adopted by the Conference of 1935 for optional use in the Methodist Church. In the introduction to the book the compilers say: 'In preparing and presenting this Book of Divine Worship we have been guided by the conviction that both traditions which Methodism has inherited, the liturgical and the free, have elements of value which should be carefully preserved and blended.'

In the opinion of many who are qualified to judge, Methodist worship has deteriorated in quality during the last fifty years. The churches which use 'Morning Prayer' have decreased in number, and the use of Canticles and

98 METHODIST WORSHIP

Psalms is also much less general than it was. The practice of kneeling is little observed, and there is a general decline in reverence and order. The ideal Sunday morning service would be one in which the Holy Communion was central, preceded by the ministry of the Word, which could prepare the minds of the worshippers for a worthy reception of the sacrament. But such an ideal could only be slowly put into practice. Dr. Rattenbury has offered the following suggestions for the improvement of morning worship.[28]

1. Reconsider the desirability of *regular* children's sermons.

2. Restore two Lessons and use the Canticles and Psalms printed at the back of the *Hymn Book*.

3. Cultivate a more scientific use of hymns, so that the four elements of public worship which Wesley described as Deprecation, Petition, Praise, and Intercession, may all have their place.

4. Observe the Christian Year, for nothing so roots worship in fact.

5. Cultivate intervals of silence.

6. Give a place for the vocal prayers and responses of the people.

The ideal service for Methodism on Sunday evenings is the evangelistic preaching service, with its object the conversion of sinners. But there are difficulties in the way of realizing this ideal. The majority of Methodists worship in the evening, and not in the morning, and in consequence the evening service tends to be a replica of the morning worship. Nevertheless, the evangelistic note must be sounded if Methodism is to be true to its heritage. Hugh Price Hughes, who combined the fervour of an evangelist with a love for ordered worship, once said:

[28] See *Vital Elements in Public Worship*, pp. 121-5.

'There is nothing I more earnestly desire, than that Methodism should be sufficiently elastic and comprehensive to satisfy every legitimate method of Christian worship.'

In a forthright article on 'The Shape of the Methodists' contributed anonymously to the *Presbyter*,[29] the writer says: 'The hymns of Charles Wesley remain, despite all transmogrifications, the greatest single element in a hymn-book which has its special place in the life of the Church, and although overlaid by nineteenth-century Nonconformity, enough persists even in the present affection of the Church to inspire and to rebuke. The Communion Service is the precious and treasured link with Anglicanism and with the devotion of many centuries: in the Covenant Service (even in its present mangled form) there is a fragment of noble liturgical writing. The present *Book of Offices* leaves no room for complacency: a number of mercifully occasional services are very second rate, while the changes in many historic services, notably the order of Baptism, are witness to serious theological confusion and impoverishment in recent times. The hacking-out of fine sentences to suit, in many cases, an ephemeral theological fashion, has had lamentable results, for it is a thousand times easier to get a sentence excised than to get it put back again once it has been omitted. When one studies the changes in offices and hymn-book over the last century the impression grows that too many great and good things have been lost, and that far too much that is shoddy and unworthy has been allowed to intrude, and one wonders whether a coherent theological and liturgical movement can grow which can win the friendly attention of our people and make out its case that its recommendations are in line with our genius and our development.'

In the report of a Commission on *The Message and*

[29] May 1946, pp. 16-25.

Mission of Methodism issued by the Conference of 1946, there is an interesting appendix on 'The Ordering of Methodist Worship'.[30] After stating that Methodist worship is based upon certain structural principles derived from the Reformation, which are then enumerated, the Report goes on to suggest that there is need to reconsider what are often wrongly described as mere matters of form. It points out that many Methodist services lack structure, and are made up of a number of unrelated items without any unifying principle. It calls for careful attention to be paid to the content, language, and form of prayers, allowing room for the congregation to make a verbal response. The value of corporate silence is stressed, and the need to review the whole service in the light of the varying types of people that make up a congregation.

One of the closing paragraphs in this appendix may be quoted as a suitable ending to this general survey of the subject of Methodist worship, before passing on to a consideration of its distinctive services, its doctrine of the sacraments, and its use of hymns in worship.

'The time is ripe for making experimental changes in the ordering of public worship. Methodism is a Free Church and in the spirit of the Reformation and of John Wesley, we have an opportunity of creating forms of worship through which the Eternal Gospel in all its richness and relevance may reach the men and women of our time. Because we are a Free Church, we are not bound by the past. For that reason also, the inheritance of the Church Universal is ours to be used to the glory of God.'

DISTINCTIVE METHODIST SERVICES

In the early days, as we have already seen, a Methodist service was not regarded as complete in itself, but was a

[30] pp. 52-4.

THE METHODIST CHURCH

supplement to the liturgy, sermon, and sacraments of the parish Church. Hours of Methodist services were so arranged as to give worshippers the chance of attending both; and John Wesley was very chary of allowing his followers to think of their meetings, even when a sermon was preached, as being in any way a substitute for the services of the Established Church. Accordingly, various characteristic Methodist services came into being, sometimes almost by accident. In each case the purpose was to give a richer fellowship than was supplied in the sometimes gabbled Liturgy of the parish Church, and to impress upon members the personal nature of religion.

The power-house of each little meeting-place was its class-meeting or the inner circle of the band-meeting. Scripture-reading and exposition, prayer, and personal testimony, together with the discipline of close examination of the spiritual state of each member by the leader and the giving of appropriate advice to each, were here coupled with the hymn-singing which Methodism was rapidly popularizing as one of the most valuable forms of religious worship. When the Society as a whole met together on the Sunday the main item was the sermon. It was what would be called today a 'preaching-service'. The Methodist emphasis on the sermon has arisen partly from the fact that it was assumed that worshippers would also take part in liturgical worship at their parish Church. On weekdays there was a short service for prayer and Bible teaching, intended for people on their way to work at 5 a.m. The first mention of this is in the *Journal* for 14th January 1740.[31] 'I began expounding the Scriptures in order at the New Room [Bristol] at six in the morning; by which means many more attend the College (i.e. the Cathedral on College Green) prayers (which immediately follow), than ever before.' Later on

[31] Vol. II, p. 332.

the time was altered to 5 a.m. These daily services were, at the outset, intended for teaching rather than for preaching. They presuppose a working-day which began much earlier in the morning—at six or seven o'clock.

Some other special occasional services were arranged by Wesley—'Letter Days', when accounts of religious progress up and down the country would be read out; 'Intercession Days', prayer-meetings with a particular purpose; but the best known are the Love-feast, the Watch-nights, and the Covenant Services. Of these latter two were borrowed from the Early Church, by way of the Moravians, and the other had its source in English Puritanism.

In *A Plain Account of the People Called Methodists*, Wesley gives this statement concerning the institution of the Love-feast among the Societies: 'In order to increase in them a grateful sense of all God's mercies, I desired that, one evening in a quarter, all the men in Band, on a second, all the women, would meet; and on a third, both men and women together; that we might together "eat bread", as the ancient Christians did, "with gladness and singleness of heart". At these Love-feasts (so we termed them, retaining the name, as well as the thing, which was in use from the beginning) our food is only a little plain cake and water. But we seldom return from them without being fed, not only with the "meat which perisheth", but with "that which endureth to everlasting life".'[32]

The Love-feasts had been instituted by the Moravians in imitation of the Agape or Love-feasts held in the early Christian Church, in some places as late as the fourth century. There they had been sometimes spoiled by selfishness and gluttony. In their revived form this was impossible. Plain cake and water, the elements of a simple meal, were distributed to all present and taken by them

[32] *Wesley's Works*, Vol. VIII, pp. 258-9.

as members of one family united by love to Christ. This was followed by testimonies concerning His love to them and theirs to Him, interspersed with songs of praise.[33] An entry in Wesley's *Journal*[34] on New Year's Day 1739 is the first reference to these gatherings: 'Mr. Hall, Kinchin, Ingham, Whitefield, Hutchins, and my brother Charles were present at our Love-feast in Fetter Lane, with about sixty of our brethren. About three in the morning, as we were continuing instant in prayer, the power of God came mightily upon us, insomuch that many cried out for exceeding joy, and many fell to the ground. As soon as we were recovered a little from that awe and amazement at the presence of His majesty, we broke out with one voice, "We praise Thee, O God; we acknowledge Thee to be the Lord".' An interesting feature about this gathering is that seven clergymen of the Church of England were present.

For many years afterwards Wesley conducted Love-feasts, on which notes are found in his *Journal* and *Diaries*. His habit seems to have been to hold one for men and one for women each month. Until 1748 only members of the Bands were admitted to the gatherings. Twenty-one years after the first Love-feast at Fetter Lane, Wesley writes in his *Journal*[35] for 9th December 1759: 'I had, for the first time, a Love-feast for the whole Society.' Members of society were admitted on producing their quarterly ticket of membership. Others might receive the written permission of the preacher to attend.

It is interesting to note that in the worship of the early English Puritans we find records of Love-feasts. They were a feature of the Church life of the early Separatists. In 1568 we are informed: 'About a week ago they discovered a newly invented sect, called by those who belong

---

[33] See R. Lee Cole, *Lovefeasts*, p. 268-9.   [34] Vol. II, pp. 121-5.
[35] Vol. IV, p. 361.

to it "the pure or stainless religion". They met to the number of one hundred and fifty in a house where their preacher used half of a tub for a pulpit, and was girded with a white cloth. Each one brought with him whatever food he had to eat, and the leaders divided money amongst those who were poorer, saying that they imitated the life of the apostles and refused to enter the temples to partake of the Lord's Supper, as it was a papistical ceremony.'[36]

There is evidence that Love-feasts were practised by the English Anabaptists, as a general feature in their communities. The Church Record of the Warboys Congregation has this entry for the year 1655: 'The order of Love-feasts agreed upon, to be before the Lord's Supper; because the ancient Churches did practise it, and for unity with other Churches near to us.'[37] This minute seems to imply that the custom was in general use among the Baptists of that day. There is also evidence of the use of the custom among London 'sectaries' in the days of the Commonwealth.

In the principal Methodist societies a Love-feast was held every quarter at the close of the Sunday morning or evening service, but in smaller places only once a year, and in modern Methodism it is almost unknown. Crowther in his *History of the Wesleyan Methodists*[38] published in 1815 describes the Love-feasts thus: 'The Love-feast is both begun and ended by singing and prayers, a travelling preacher presiding. The time is chiefly taken up in relating Christian experience. Any person may speak who chooses. They are generally very agreeable, edifying, and refreshing seasons. They tend to promote piety, mutual affection, and zeal. A collection is made, the first object of which is to pay for the bread

[36] Quoted by Horton Davies, *Worship of the English Puritans*, p. 93.
[37] Quoted op. cit., p. 245. [38] p. 283.

used on the occasion; and the surplus is divided among the poor members of the society where the Love-feast is held.'

In *A Plain Account* Wesley also gives a statement of the origin of the Watch-night. He writes: 'About this time I was informed that several persons in Kingswood frequently met together at the school; and, when they could spare the time, spent the greater part of the night in prayer, and praise, and thanksgiving. Some advised me to put an end to this; but, upon weighing the thing thoroughly, and comparing it with the practice of the ancient Christians, I could see no cause to forbid it. Rather, I believed it might be made of more general use. So I sent them word, I designed to watch with them on the Friday nearest the full moon, that we might have light thither and back again. I gave public notice of this the Sunday before, and withal that I intended to preach; desiring they, and they only, would meet me there, who could do it without prejudice to their business or families. On Friday abundance of people came. I began preaching between eight and nine; and we continued a little beyond the noon of night, singing, praying, and praising God. This we have continued to do once a month ever since, in Bristol, London, and Newcastle, as well as Kingswood; and exceeding great are the blessings we have found therein. It has generally been an extremely solemn season; when the Word of God sunk deep into the heart. . . .'[39]

It is difficult to decide when the first Methodist Watch-night Service took place. Friday 12th March 1742 is the most likely date. The Methodist Watch-night should be distinguished from the Moravian in that the former was held 'monthly on the Friday nearest the full moon'. Those held on the last nights of 1739 and 1740 were probably Moravian. When Wesley says in the passage just quoted from *A Plain Account* 'about this time', he is

[39] *Wesley's Works*, Vol. VIII, pp. 246-7.

referring to the origin of the class-meeting which he has just described. The date of that is known to be 15th February 1742. On Friday 9th April 1742 Wesley records: 'We had the first watch-night in London.' It may be assumed that at some time between those two dates the watch-night was introduced. On 12th March 1742 there is this entry in the *Journal*:[40] 'Our Lord was gloriously present with us at the watch-night, so that my voice was lost in the cries of the people. After midnight, about a hundred of us walked home together, singing and rejoicing, and praising God.' Myles's *History*[41] says that the watch-night was substituted by Wesley for the wild carousals of the Kingswood miners on Saturday nights in their unconverted days. Wesley saw the value of the annual Moravian Watch-night, but made it more frequent to meet the needs of his converts. Eventually the more Moravian annual Watch-night, held on the last night of the year, a custom which has spread to many of the other Churches, was left, and the monthly meeting passed away.

A clergyman of Cork named Baily made an attack on Wesley's activities to which Wesley replied in a letter: 'You charge me ... with holding "midnight assemblies". Sir, did you never see the word "Vigil" in your *Common Prayer Book*? Do you know what it means? If not, permit me to tell you that it was customary with the ancient Christians to spend whole nights in prayer, and that these nights were termed *Vigiliae*, or Vigils. Therefore, for spending a part of some nights in this manner, in public and solemn prayer, we have not only the authority of our own national Church, but of the universal Church in the earliest ages.'[42]

Two Watch-night hymns by Charles Wesley appear in *Hymns and Sacred Poems*, issued in 1742, which indicate

[40] Vol. II, p. 534. [41] p. 56.
[42] *Letters of John Wesley*, Vol. III, p. 287.

the mood in which the people should assemble at such a service. One of them begins:

> *Oft have we passed the guilty night*
> *In revellings and frantic mirth,*

words very appropriate for the Kingswood miners, though later generations hesitated to make such a confession and the first line was changed to 'How many pass the guilty night'. The second verse is as follows:

> *We will not close our wakeful eyes,*
> *We will not let our eyelids sleep,*
> *But humbly lift them to the skies,*
> *And all a solemn vigil keep;*
> *So many years on sin bestowed,*
> *Can we not watch one night for God?*

Wesley has left an account in his *Journal* of the institution of the Covenant Service. On Wednesday 6th August 1755 he writes: 'I mentioned to the congregation another means of increasing serious religion, which had been frequently practised by our forefathers, and attended with eminent blessing; namely, the joining in a covenant to serve God with all our heart and with all our soul. I explained this for several mornings following, and on Friday many of us kept a fast unto the Lord, beseeching him to give us wisdom and strength to promise unto the Lord our God and keep it.'[43] Then on the 11th he writes: 'I explained once more the nature of such an engagement, and the manner of doing it acceptably to God. At six in the evening we met for that purpose at the French church in Spitalfields. After I had recited the tenor of the covenant proposed, in the words of that blessed man, Richard Alleine, all the people stood up, in testimony of assent, to the number of about eighteen hundred persons. Such a

[43] op. cit., Vol. IV, p. 126.

night I scarce ever saw before. Surely the fruit of it shall remain for ever.'[44] In April 1757 he writes in the *Journal*: 'On Good Friday, in the evening, at the meeting of the Society, God was eminently present with us. I read over and enlarged upon Joseph Alleine's *Directions for a Thorough Conversion to God*.'[45] The service for the renewal of the Covenant was held on the following Monday at Spitalfields, with about twelve hundred people present. 'At half-hour after nine, God broke in mightily upon the congregation.'

There are many references in the *Journal* to the blessing which attended this service whenever it was held. It may be claimed that Methodism has contributed nothing more notable to the worship of the Church than the Covenant Service. From time to time the form has been altered, but the central purpose and substance have remained and kept hold of the affections and imagination of the people called Methodists. The service is intended to mark a new turning back from sin, a fresh acceptance of God's purposes for His people and a renewal of the bond between their souls and God. The strength of the service stands in its equal stress on the emotions and ethics. The heart is warmed anew toward God, as is right; but the will is also stirred up to right living, without which none can see God.

Wesley found scriptural warrant for the Covenant Service in passages like Deuteronomy 26^{17-18}, Jeremiah 31^{31-4}, and Ezekiel 16^{60}. The practice of making covenants with God originated in the Covenant theology popular among the Puritan theologians. The Presbyterian Covenants were national, the most notable example being the Solemn League and Covenant of 1643. The Covenants among the Congregationalists were confined to the local church. They based their church-life on the

[44] op. cit., Vol. IV, p. 126.   [45] ibid., p. 200.

church-covenant, a solemn agreement made between the members of each 'gathered' church, by which they determined the nature of its government.

The service used by Wesley had two parts. The first contained the 'Directions' by which members were prepared to make their Covenant. The second was the Covenant itself, which in its original form begins: 'O most dreadful God, for the passion of Thy Son, I beseech Thee to accept of Thy poor prodigal . . .' and ended: 'And the Covenant which I have made on earth, let it be ratified in heaven.' The Reverend Frederick Hunter in an article in the *Wesley Historical Society Proceedings* for June 1940 has discussed in some detail the origins of the Covenant service. He assigns the second part of the service to a young Presbyterian minister, Joseph Alleine, who about 1658 began to use the Covenant for young converts. It was published after his death in 1672 in his *Alarm to Unconverted Sinners*. The first part of the service was written by Richard Alleine, the father-in-law of Joseph. After the Restoration of 1660, the Presbyterians became Dissenters, and persecution followed. In 1663 Richard Alleine published his *Vindiciae Pietatis*, or *Vindication of Godliness*. At the end of his defence of Puritanism, he gives five directions to the ungodly in order to bring them to a godly life, the fifth urging them to make a formal Covenant with God. He then gives Joseph Alleine's converts' Covenant. These five directions were used by Wesley as the introductory part of his service, as a preparation for the making of the Covenant. The practice of making covenants became very common between the Restoration and 1700, and there is evidence that Alleine's Covenant was widely used in the founding of congregations in 1672.

The Covenant Service was held on New Year's Day in 1748, and 1766, and each year from 1770 to 1778, except 1774. From 1782 onward Wesley held it on the first

Sunday in the year. The first printed Methodist Covenant Service was issued by Thomas Lee on 10th December 1779. The inadequacies of this booklet led Wesley to issue his first edition of the service in 1780. It was for public rather than private use. Charles Wesley's hymn, 'Come, let us use the grace divine', published in 1762 brings out the corporate nature of the Covenant, as being the act of the whole society or church. Although a corporate act, it also remained a completely personal act. So at the first service, in 1755, the people signified their assent by standing, and in Wesley's printed service, he inserted Joseph Alleine's advice that the Covenant should be signed.

The present 'Order of Service for such as would enter into or renew their Covenant with God, for use on the first Sunday of the year' has these words by way of preface: 'On 25th December 1747 John Wesley strongly urged the Methodists to renew their Covenant with God. His first Covenant Service was held in the French Church at Spitalfields, on 11th August 1755, when he recited the words of "that blessed man Richard Alleine", which he published that year in the *Christian Library*. Wesley issued this as a pamphlet in 1780, and the form was used without alteration for nearly a century. Various modifications were then made, till a form was prepared which gave the people a larger share in the devotions. That form has now been revised with a deep sense of the importance of a service which has been a fruitful source of blessing to Methodism ever since 1755.'[46]

After the hymn, 'Come, let us use the grace divine', and the Collect for Purity and the Lord's Prayer, and the reading of John 15$^{1-8}$, there follows a brief explanation of the two-sided nature of the Covenant. Then comes an act of Adoration and Thanksgiving, followed by a call to

[46] *The Book of Offices.*

self-examination, and a prayer of Confession. This leads to the taking of the Covenant itself, when the people are called to take upon them the yoke of Christ and to bind themselves with willing bonds to their covenant God. Minister and people say these words together: 'I am no longer my own, but Thine. Put me to what Thou wilt, rank me with whom Thou wilt; put me to doing, put me to suffering; let me be employed for Thee or laid aside for Thee, exalted for Thee or brought low for Thee; let me be full, let me be empty; let me have all things, let me have nothing; I freely and heartily yield all things to Thy pleasure and disposal. And now, O glorious and blessed God, Father, Son and Holy Spirit, Thou art mine, and I am Thine. So be it. And the Covenant which I have made on earth, let it be ratified in heaven. Amen.'

This service is used in every Methodist Church on the first Sunday in the New Year, and is followed by the Holy Communion. All these services which are distinctive of Methodism serve to emphasize what is still its glory—the warmth of Christian fellowship. They have proved useful and effective in bringing sinners to God and in confirming the devotion of believers.

THE METHODIST DOCTRINE OF BAPTISM

There is very little on the subject of Baptism in the fourteen volumes of *Wesley's Works*. He revised and reissued under his own name in 1756 the treatise on the subject which his father had published more than half a century before and which teaches 'baptismal regeneration' as it was taught by the Puritan divines of the Church of England. Elsewhere all that Wesley says apart from two sentences in his *Notes on the New Testament* (Acts 22[16], John 3[5]) is in two sermons and in his *Farther Appeal to Men of Reason and Religion*. He allows that infants are made children of God by baptism. 'It is certain our Church supposes that all who are baptized in their infancy are at the same time born again: and it is allowed that the whole office for the Baptism of Infants proceeds upon this supposition. Nor is it an objection of any weight against this, that we cannot comprehend how this work can be wrought in infants. For neither can we comprehend how it is wrought in a person of riper years.[47] It is true that in the same sermon Wesley lays it down that baptism and the new birth are not one and the same thing, the one being an external and the other an internal work, and he admits that there may be the outward sign where there is not the inward grace. He also asserts that 'it is sure all of riper years who are baptized are not at the same time born again'.[48]

In his sermon on 'The Marks of the New Birth' Wesley only refers to the subject to rebut the pretensions of those who claimed to be Christians on the strength of their baptism as infants. He allows that as infants they were regenerated, but asks repeatedly of what avail that fact can be in the case of those who are now beyond question living godless lives. In the *Farther Appeal* he uses almost identical language in one place,[49] while in another he says that 'our Church supposes infants to be justified in baptism, although they cannot then either believe or repent'.[50]

His position is set forth more fully in the *Treatise on Baptism*[51] which has already been mentioned. There he gives the benefits we receive in baptism as follows: 1. 'Washing away the guilt of original sin [infants are included because they have original sin, though if they die before committing actual sin they are saved, as the Prayer Book says]; 2. By baptism we enter into covenant with God;

[47] *Wesley's Works*, Vol. VI, p. 69.   [48] ibid.   [49] ibid., Vol. VIII, p. 48.
[50] ibid., p. 52.   [51] ibid., Vol. X, pp. 181-93.

3. By baptism we are admitted into the Church [compared with circumcision]; 4. By water . . . as a means, the water of baptism, we are regenerated or born again.' It is not ascribed to the 'outward washing but to the inward grace which, added thereto, makes it a sacrament'. 5. 'We are made heirs of the kingdom of heaven.' In the fourth section of this treatise Wesley lays down the grounds of infant baptism and answers objections to it. The chief grounds are that 'infants need to be washed from original sin; therefore they are proper subjects of baptism'; and that infants are capable of making a covenant and coming to Christ and therefore have a right to baptism which is the seal of the covenant. The most serious difficulty he has to meet is the absence of faith and repentance, which he disposes of by pointing out the similar difficulty in the rite of circumcision.

Wesley's position is fairly clear. Regeneration or being born again is annexed to baptism in the sense that the rite is the seal of an inward change. Infants, who are baptized because they need washing from the guilt of original sin, may be regarded as regenerated in baptism itself. With this may be compared a baptismal hymn by Charles Wesley:

> *Born in the dregs of sin and time,*
>   *These darkest, last, apostate days,*
> *Burdened with Adam's curse and crime,*
>   *Thou in Thy mercy's arms embrace,*
> *And wash out all her guilty load,*
> *And quench the brand in Jesus' blood.*

And in a later verse:

> *Now to this favoured babe be given,*
> *Pardon, and holiness, and heaven.*[52]

---

[52] *Poetical Works of John and Charles Wesley*, Vol. VII, No. 62.

But as Dr. Sugden points out in his discussion of the question this position was disputed in Methodism from the very first and there are signs that Wesley himself moved away from it.[53] The *Sunday Service of the Methodists* (1784 and 1786) omitted the phrases on regeneration which are used in *The Book of Common Prayer*. The Methodist Articles of Religion prepared by Wesley for the American Methodists contain one on baptism in which all that is taught as to the nature of baptism is that, besides being a sign of the Christian profession, it is also a sign of regeneration or the new birth. Not a word is said about baptism as an instrument or about the effects of baptism. This Article proves that Wesley had in 1784 concluded not to insist on the doctrine of baptismal regeneration. When the *Wesleyan Book of Offices* was revised in 1882 all phrases that might suggest that the infant was born again in baptism were omitted. From the preamble, John 3⁵ and the petition 'that he may be baptized not only with water but also with the Holy Ghost' were omitted; the Four Prayers ('O merciful God, grant that the old Adam', etc.) were placed after instead of before the administration; and references to and prayers for parents were scattered throughout the Service. The Conference 'Memorandum on Infant Baptism' of 1936[54] makes no reference to 'washing from sin' and the Order of Service for the Baptism of Infants in the present *Book of Offices* likewise ignores it. It would seem that in order to avoid a false and unscriptural statement of baptismal regeneration, successive generations of Methodists have lost sight of a highly scriptural feature of the sacrament. Nearly seventy years ago Dr. George Osborn, addressing the Wesleyan Conference, said: 'I cannot think that we as a community realize the full significance of infant baptism.' Philip Henry (who

---

[53] *Standard Sermons of John Wesley*, Vol. I, pp. 280-2.
[54] *Minutes of Conference*, pp. 400-1.

was John Wesley's pattern in family devotion) said: 'If infant baptism were more improved it would be less disputed.' About the same time, while the Wesleyan Conference was engaged in revising the Baptismal Office, a leading article in the *Methodist Recorder* for 23rd August 1878 contained these words: 'Infant Baptism has degenerated in many instances into mere christening. The Covenant character of the ordinance is often lost sight of. It is associated with no peculiar Church privileges: it leads to no practical results; nothing is sought or expected from it; no action is taken upon it; it stands detached and isolated—a rite once administered, but connected with no Church position to which it is the introduction, with no religious privileges and obligations to which it is the sign and seal. It is virtually degraded into a mere formality, a mere ceremony carrying no high and solemn import. The Anglo-Catholics ascribe to it a magical virtue *ex opere operato*: the Baptists deny to it all relevancy, any validity whatever. The former make it everything, the latter nothing. Can we suppose that if there had been in the Churches of this country a theory of Baptism, and a corresponding practice, in harmony with the teaching of the New Testament and with the usage of the primitive Church, either the doctrine of baptismal regeneration on the one hand, or the doctrine of the utter invalidity and worthlessness of infant baptism on the other, would have gained such prevalence? We must find the remedy and apply it.'

The remedy has not been found yet. The Methodist beliefs on this subject lack unity and their practice lacks uniformity. According to Sugden, the 'danger in Methodism has not been in the direction of overestimating the value of this sacrament', but in 'our perfunctoriness in the administration of it, and our subsequent failure to look after our baptized children'. He suggests that Methodists have erred in 'dropping the rite of Confirmation without substituting for it some solemn service at which our baptized children will consciously take upon themselves the vows made for them at their baptism'. The 'Memorandum on Infant Baptism' already referred to begins by stating the origin and catholicity of the sacrament, and goes on to explain how Infant Baptism arose and the sacramental differences between it and Adult Baptism. It describes Infant Baptism as the sacrament of initiation into the Church on earth and a symbol of universal grace. It states what Baptism symbolizes for the Church and for the parents. Responsibility for the child is said to be an essential element in the Baptismal Service. The Memorandum ends with these words. 'We assert in common with the general body of the Church of Christ, that a solemn obligation to Christ, the Church, and the child rests upon parents to present their children to Christ in Baptism, and thus to honour the ancient ordinance whereby they are joined to the visible community of Christ's people.'[55]

This exposition has nothing to say about that aspect of the rite which is traditionally expressed by 'washing from sin', neither is there any reference to it in the present Order of Service. This service is based largely on the *Book of Common Prayer* of 1662 by way of the *Book of Public Prayers and Services for the use of the People called Methodists* of 1882. A comparison of the services will show clearly differences in aim.[56]

The service begins with an exhortation to the people in which the ministry of Christ to the child is explained and the corresponding duty of ministry which falls upon the Church and the parents. This ministry is a consequence of the promise of His redeeming grace and we are

[55] *Minutes of Conference*, p. 401.
[56] Kenneth Grayston, 'On the Order of Service for Baptism of Infants', *London Quarterly and Holborn Review*, July 1944, p. 210ff.

to believe that Christ will give the Holy Spirit so that the child may be a partaker of His Kingdom. *The Book of Common Prayer* expounds the doctrine of redeeming grace in these terms: 'Forasmuch as all men are conceived and born in sin; and that our Saviour Christ saith, None can enter into the kingdom of God except he be regenerate and born anew of water and the Holy Ghost,' prayer is offered that the child may be granted 'that thing which by nature he cannot have', namely, 'remission of his sins by spiritual regeneration'. For this purpose God, by the baptism of Christ, sanctified 'water to the mystical washing away of sin'. The *Methodist Prayer Book*, 1882, partly remodels these prayers so as to omit the references to mystical washing but it retains the phrase 'Give the Holy Spirit to this infant that he may be born again', and 'wash him and sanctify him with the Holy Ghost, that, he, being delivered from Thy wrath, may be received into the ark of Christ's Church'.

There follows an exhortation to the parents which stresses the dedication of the child as a disciple and the ministry of parents and Church. The *Prayer Book* emphasizes his cleansing and sanctification. Then come questions addressed to the parents which require them to promise a Christian home, and access to the teaching and worship of the Church. In the *Prayer Book* the godparents are required to renounce the devil and all his works, as sureties for the child. The congregation is asked to guarantee to maintain the fellowship of worship and service.

Next comes a prayer of intercession for the child which mainly reproduces that in the *Prayer Book*, but instead of the words 'and enjoy the everlasting benediction of the heavenly washing' it substitutes 'ever remain Christ's true disciple'. The prayer of intercession for the home which follows comes from the 1928 *Prayer Book*, where it is placed at the end of the service after the baptism. After prayer for the Holy Spirit to be given to the parents the rite of baptism is administered according to the Anglican form. The Methodist service omits the sign of the cross and the words which follow it in *The Book of Common Prayer*, 'in token that hereafter he shall not be ashamed to confess the faith of Christ crucified, and manfully to fight under his banner, against sin, the world, and the devil'. The Benediction is the one used in the 1928 *Prayer Book*. Then come various petitions, for the gift of the Holy Spirit, to the child, for his growth in the spiritual life, for his victory over the world, the flesh, and the devil, and finally for the parents and the congregation. The service ends with the Grace.

A study of this service reveals that Baptism is interpreted as a sign of a child's admission to the fellowship of Christ's Church, of the privileges of discipleship, and of the gift of the Holy Spirit. A central place in the service is given to the responsibility of the parents and of the Church. It is not true as many believe that Baptism is a service for the parents or that they occupy a more important place than the child. Their importance is derived from him.

The only reference to conquest of sin occurs in two of the petitions at the close of the service: 'Grant that all things belonging to the flesh may die in him, and that all things belonging to the Spirit may live and grow in him.' 'Grant that he may have power and strength to have victory, and to triumph over the world, the flesh, and the devil.' In *The Book of Common Prayer* these petitions are offered before the baptism and the reason may be seen from the following quotations: 'Seeing now . . . that this child is regenerate and grafted into the body of Christ's Church', and 'We yield Thee hearty thanks . . . that it hath pleased Thee to regenerate this infant with Thy Holy Spirit to receive him for Thine own child, by adoption, and to incorporate him into Thy holy Church'. 'In the *Methodist Book of Offices* the petitions are transferred to the present position to show (*a*) that we do not think that the *mere* act of baptism secures their answer and (*b*) that baptism is the *beginning* of a process and not itself a completed whole. *The Book of Common Prayer* admits this by its service of Confirmation; but here it is clearly brought out in the Baptism itself.'[57] Yet it would seem to be a serious omission that Baptism is not also expounded as a sign of God's promise of the conquest of sin.

It is necessary to remember that the child is born into a fallen world, and no less than the adult, he is entitled to the sign that God, through the sacrifice of Christ, has refused to let this be a barrier between us and Him. The sign declares that God's grace sets the child at once within the sphere of His personal fellowship despite the fallen nature of man. Regeneration is a promise of which baptism is the pledge. When the Church baptizes a child it seals upon him the promise of the Gospel. When he is able to exercise conscious faith he will take his part in the other Gospel sacrament that he may continue to enjoy the forgiveness pledged to him in his baptism. So, to quote Methodism's greatest theologian, Dr. W. B. Pope: 'The baptism of the children of believing parents is a sign of the washing away of original guilt and a seal of their adoption into the family of God, a sign of the regeneration which their nature needs, and a seal of its impartation in God's good time.'[58]

NOTE: In theory what has been said here of the Methodist doctrine of Baptism applies only to the children of

---

[57] Kenneth Grayston, op. cit., p. 212, and cf. W. F. Flemington, *The New Testament Doctrines of Baptism*, p. 140.
[58] *Compendium of Christian Theology*, Vol. III, pp. 317-18.

believing parents, but in practice many infants are baptized in our Churches whose parents are neither members nor adherents of the Church, and there is danger of a superstitious or magical element entering into the use of the Sacrament. There is in the Methodist *Book of Offices* an order of service for the 'Baptism of such as are of riper years'.

In the Wesleyan Methodist Church the administration of the sacrament was confined to the travelling preachers. In 1811 Conference directed the superintendent of a circuit to take care 'that no person be permitted to administer the sacraments ... but a travelling preacher in full connexion'. The absolute nature of this rule was confirmed by a regulation of 1829 which extended permission to Junior Preachers to baptize, but only where children could not be brought to Church or in circumstances of great emergency. This remained the rule throughout the history of Wesleyan Methodism. The order of service used was that of the Church of England as agreed in the Plan of Pacification and repeated in 1840. Later, liberty was granted 'to give out hymns, to use exhortation, and extemporary prayer' (1869) and by 1882 it had been found advisable to prepare a 'revision of the Liturgy and *Book of Offices*', but in adopting the new order of service it was resolved that 'the Conference does not prohibit the use of any forms which have heretofore been approved by the Conference'.

At first the administration of Baptism was intended 'only for the members of our own society', but this was soon extended to include not only the children of members but also 'those of our regular hearers'. It was to be administered, if possible, 'in the public congregation', and 'not at the close of the public service, but before the sermon' (1840). Among the other branches of the

Methodist Church the administration of Baptism was never confined solely to the ministers. Since Methodist Union in 1932 no specific statement has been made by Conference on this point. In the Order of Service for the Ordination of Candidates it is made very clear that they are ordained to the ministry of the Word and of the Sacraments—the *two*—and a probationer receives a dispensation to administer them, before which he has no authority to administer either.[59]

THE METHODIST DOCTRINE OF HOLY COMMUNION

Three affirmations may be made of Methodist doctrine in general. First, that it is essentially evangelical; second, that it is based upon the divine revelation recorded in the scriptures; and third, that it is interpreted in *Wesley's Notes on the New Testament* and the first four volumes of his *Sermons*. The final authority for a doctrinal definition is the Methodist Conference; but the Conference has no power to initiate doctrine; it can only interpret. The Methodist attitude to Holy Communion is determined by these standards, that is to say, it is evangelical in outlook, in harmony with the Scriptures, in line with the teaching of Wesley, and is given expression through an order or form issued with the authority of the Conference. It may be useful to consider these points sucessively.[60]

1. *The Evangelical Doctrine.* It is important to observe that the evangelical tradition, which is based on the Reformed doctrine, while rejecting Roman sacramental views acknowledges the sacramental character of the

[59] Norman W. Mumford, 'The Administration of the Sacrament of Baptism in the Methodist Church', *London Quarterly and Holborn Review*, April 1947, pp. 113-19.

[60] I am indebted in this section to an article by A. Gordon James, *London Quarterly and Holborn Review*, January 1940, pp. 51-60; and to an Essay by E. Gordon Rupp, p. 113. *The Holy Communion:* a Symposium in addition to other books mentioned.

Christian religion. It affirms that through material forms and symbols man can be made aware of the presence of God. It is not denied that God can and does communicate with the human spirit directly, and intuitively; yet it is acknowledged that in a material world, means of grace are necessary if men are to apprehend spiritual reality. The final ground of this belief is the doctrine of the Incarnation. Christianity is a religion of the Word made flesh, that is, a sacramental religion, which is by no means the same as a sacerdotal religion. Evangelicalism rejects sacerdotalism, but it does not repudiate the sacramental principle, which is fundamental to Christian faith.

The evangelical doctrine of Holy Communion admits that, to the eye of faith, Christ is present in a very real sense in the act of Communion. Zwingli, who is generally supposed to have taught that the observance of the Lord's Supper is nothing but a commemorative act, held that Christ is objectively present, WITH, though not IN the bread and wine.[61] Calvin held a real, though spiritual feeding upon the body and blood of Christ.[62] He says in the *Institutes*, IV.xvii.10: 'That sacred communion of flesh and blood by which Christ transfuses His life into us, just as if it penetrated our bones and marrow, He testifies and seals in the supper.' Wesley declares, in a sermon on 'The Means of Grace' included in the doctrinal standards of the Methodist Church: 'Is not the eating of that bread, and the drinking of that cup, the outward, visible means, whereby God conveys into our souls all that spiritual grace, that righteousness, and peace, and joy in the Holy Ghost, which were purchased by the body of Christ once broken, and the blood of Christ once shed, for us? Let all, therefore, who truly desire the grace of God, eat of that bread, and drink of that cup.'[63]

---

[61] cf. W. B. Pope, *Compendium of Christian Theology*, Vol. III, p. 332.
[62] See A. Dakin, *Calvinism*, pp. 121-2.   [63] *Wesley's Works*, Vol. V, p. 183.

THE METHODIST CHURCH

2. *The New Testament.* It may be admitted that various interpretations of the New Testament account of the institution of the Lord's Supper are possible. But no one will deny that the words 'This is my body' and 'This is my blood' are an authentic part of the record. If, therefore, these words are incorporated in any service of Holy Communion, it cannot be objected that such a service is out of harmony with New Testament teaching, unless a false and unscriptural value is attached to them. In *The Book of Offices* issued with the authority of the Methodist Conference, the prayer which guards the approach to the Table of the Lord contains the following explanatory sentences, indicating the manner in which Scripture is used and the meaning attached to 'body' and 'blood' in this connexion: ' . . . and grant that we receiving these Thy creatures of bread and wine, according to Thy Son our Saviour Jesus Christ's holy institution, in remembrance of His death and passion, may be partakers of His most blessed Body and Blood: who, in the same night that He was betrayed, took bread; and when He had given thanks, He brake it, and gave it to His disciples, saying, Take, eat; this is My Body, which is given for you; Do this in remembrance of Me. Likewise after supper He took the cup; and when He had given thanks, He gave it to them, saying, Drink ye all of this; for this is My Blood of the New Covenant, which is shed for you and for many for the remissions of sins: Do this, as oft as ye shall drink it, in remembrance of Me.'[64]

In these words scriptural warrant is claimed for the observance of Holy Communion as a means of 'partaking' the most blessed Body and Blood of our Lord, through the medium of bread and wine.

3. *The Teaching of the Wesleys.* In the *Rules of the Society*, issued by John and Charles Wesley in 1743, the members

[64] *The Book of Offices.*

are required to 'attend upon all the ordinances of God', and in a list of six such ordinances, 'The Supper of the Lord' comes third.[65] Both by precept and example Wesley continually urged the duty and blessing of the partaking of this sacrament. In 1788 he published a sermon on 'The Duty of Constant Communion' which he had written at Oxford for the use of his pupils in 1733. He says in the preface: 'I have added very little, but retrenched much; as I then used more words than I do now. But, I thank God, I have not yet seen cause to alter my sentiments in any point which is therein delivered.'[66] In the sermon he strongly protests that 'frequent' communion is inadequate: it must be 'constant'. 'No man can have any pretence to Christian piety who does not receive it, not once a month, but as often as he can.' 'He that, when he may obey the commandment if he will, does not, will have no place in the kingdom of heaven.' Wesley's diaries show that, in 1733, five years before his evangelical conversion, as a High Anglican of the non-Juror type, he communicated once a week and on holydays. In 1740 (two years after his evangelical experience) he communicated ninety-one times, that is, once in every four days. During 1782 he communicated every other day. In this, as in all his years of evangelistic toil, he was in constant travel. In the Christmas season of 1775 he writes: 'We had the Lord's Supper daily', and in the last few weeks of his life he communicated once every three days.[67]

If it be suggested that this sacramental zeal on Wesley's part was a personal idiosyncrasy and out of touch with the distinctive genius of evangelical religion, the answer must be that his followers were organized on the basis of a

[65] *Wesley's Works*, Vol. VIII, p. 261.   [66] ibid., Vol. VII, p. 140.
[67] See T. H. Barratt, 'The Place of the Lord's Supper in Early Methodism', *London Quarterly Review*, July 1923.

sacramental society. The early Methodists were both evangelical and sacramental to a remarkable degree. At a period in the history of the Anglican Church when Holy Communion was in most parish churches observed only three or four times a year, when Secker, Bishop of Oxford, could plead, in addressing his clergy in 1741, that 'a sacrament might be interposed in the long interval between Whitsuntide and Christmas', the Methodist people were communicating in multitudes every Sunday morning.[68] In preparing a constitution and Order of Worship for the Methodists in the newly-formed United States of America Wesley wrote in 1784: 'I advise the elders to administer the Supper of the Lord on every Lord's Day.' This also represents his intention, and so far as was possible, his practice in the earliest Methodist chapels in London and the provinces. In these the Sunday morning service normally consisted of the preaching of the Word and the administration of the Lord's Supper—a complete synthesis of evangelical and sacramental worship. The attendance at these Sunday morning communions forms one of the most astonishing features of the Methodist Revival. The number of communicants and the inevitable prolongation of the services caused the Wesleys serious physical exhaustion. Frequently the service lasted five hours—from ten to three o'clock. In 1743 Wesley writes: 'I found it needful for the time to come to divide the communicants into three parts, so that we might not have above six hundred at once.' At Leeds, Wesley mentions seven hundred communicants in 1779, and 1789 fifteen or sixteen hundred. At Oldham Street Chapel, Manchester, in 1781, he writes: 'I began reading prayers at ten o'clock.... At the communion was such a sight as I am persuaded was never seen at Manchester before: eleven or twelve hundred communicants

---

[68] T. Secker, *Charge Delivered to the Clergy*, p. 62.

at once, and all of them fearing God.'[69] At Bristol, Bath, Plymouth, Sheffield, Newcastle, Cork, and Dublin, he quotes figures of communicants at morning service which vary from three hundred to one thousand. This took place at a period when the Dean of St. Paul's lamented that on Easter Day 1800, there were only six communicants.

One of Wesley's preachers, John Pawson, says: 'I had now [1763] an opportunity to receive the holy sacrament among the children of God; and to see the large and deeply serious congregations that attended the chapels, the uncommon number of communicants, their devout behaviour and the order with which the whole service was conducted, was highly pleasing to me. O, how divinely pleasant, and how truly profitable, it is to wait upon God in His holy ordinances, when He is present in the power of His Spirit, and they are conducted according to His own appointment!'[70] These remarkable scenes were not confined to the towns—Wesley writes in June 1744— 'I was much pleased . . . at Redmire, when, from a village of about thirty houses, we had more than fifty communicants.'[71]

Wesley used the Lord's Supper as a means of evangelizing. He invited all sinners seeking salvation to the Table, and insisted that they would find the Saviour. In this he was doubtless influenced by the experience of his mother, who received 'the assurance of forgiveness' at the Lord's Table in August 1739. A few months later (June 1740) we find Wesley writing: 'I preached on "Do this in remembrance of me". . . . In latter times many have affirmed that the Lord's Supper is not a converting, but a confirming ordinance. Among us it has been diligently taught

[69] *Journal of John Wesley*, Vol. VI, p. 310.
[70] *Lives of Early Methodist Preachers*, Vol. IV, p. 27.
[71] *Journal of John Wesley*, Vol. III, p. 140.

that none but those who are converted, . . . who are believers in the full sense, ought to communicate. But experience shows the gross falsehood of the assertion that the Lord's Supper is not a converting ordinance. Ye are the witnesses. For many now present know, the very beginning of your conversion to God . . . was wrought at the Lord's Supper.'[72]

There is evidence of close connexion between the sacramental and converting power of the Revival. 'I preached at West Street,' writes Wesley. 'We had a glorious opportunity at the Lord's Supper; the rocks were broken in pieces.'[73] One of his preachers, James Rogers writes: 'In the beginning of December one was justified . . . when receiving the sacrament. . . . On Good Friday two men were justified under the Word, and one at the communion.'[74]

In his sermon on 'The Means of Grace' Wesley is careful to insist that 'God is above all means', and to warn his hearers against 'limiting the Almighty'. 'He can convey His grace, either in or out of any of the means which He hath appointed. . . . [The ordinance in itself], the *opus operatum*, the mere *work done*, profiteth nothing. . . . Even what God ordains conveys no grace to the soul if you trust not in Him alone.'[75]

In 1742, a book was published with this title: *A Companion for the Altar: Extracted from Thomas à Kempis*, by John Wesley, M.A. This was followed three years later by *Hymns on the Lord's Supper: by John and Charles Wesley, With a Preface concerning the Christian Sacrament and Sacrifice, extracted from Dr. Brevint.*[76] Both these books passed

[72] *Wesley's Works*, Vol. I, p. 262. [73] *Journal of John Wesley*, Vol. V, p. 99.
[74] *Lives of Early Methodist Preachers*, Vol. IV, pp. 317-18.
[75] *Wesley's Works*, Vol. V, p. 188.
[76] *Poetical Works of John and Charles Wesley*, Vol. III, pp. 181-342. (The third and some later editions have 'John and Charles Wesley, Presbyters of the Church of England', on the title page.) Printed in full in Dr. Rattenbury's *The Eucharistic Hymns of John and Charles Wesley*.

through several editions in the life-time of the Wesleys. There is no doubt that they heartily recommended the use of both books to their people.

The tract by Dr. Brevint, Dean of Lincoln, is divided into sections concerning the Sacrament, including:

As it is a memorial of the sufferings and death of Christ.
As it is a sign of present graces.
As it is a means of grace.
As it is a pledge of future glory.
As it is a sacrifice (a) a commemorative sacrifice
(b) a sacrifice of ourselves.

This tract was read by John Wesley on his voyage to America, and his brother turned it into verse, keeping very closely to the original.

The first one hundred and fifty-seven hymns are arranged to illustrate the five sections of the tract; a sixth section consists of nine hymns to be used after the Sacrament. The hymns went through eleven editions until 1825, when the Conference again recommended their use. Fourteen have survived into the present *Methodist Hymn Book*.[77]

It would seem from a careful study of the hymns that for once Charles Wesley finds himself at home with Calvin and is prepared to take refuge in a reticent agnosticism, as in Hymn No. 57:

. . . . . .

> *Who shall say how bread and wine*
> *God into man conveys!*
> How *the bread His flesh imparts*,
> How *the wine transmits His blood*,
> *Fills His faithful people's hearts*
> *With all the life of God!*

[77] They are Nos. 181, 191, 382, 566, 574, 723, 760, 761, 764, 765, 767, 771, 818, 833.

Or again in Hymn No. 92:

> *It doth not appear,*
> *His manner of working; but Jesus is here!*

The hymns are full of a sense of the spiritual presence of the Lord in the Sacrament because it is a specially appointed channel of grace. While the peculiar value of the Sacrament is emphasized, there is no denial of the validity of other means of grace.[78]

The Wesleys regarded the Sacrament as a powerful means of preaching Christ crucified just as John Owen did in his *Sacramental Discourses*. The Eucharist is a sacrifice they keep on repeating, and not only a sacrifice of praise and thanksgiving but a re-presentation in picture of the sacrifice of Calvary. That remains the 'one sacrifice for sins for ever' and can never be repeated; it can only be revivified to the believing heart:

> *The Lamb as crucified afresh*
> *Is here held out to men,*
> *The tokens of His blood and flesh*
> *Are on this table seen.*[79]

To the end of his life Wesley held that only an ordained presbyter should administer the sacraments. That conviction involved him and the Methodist people in the gravest difficulties. If he were to be consistent with that belief he could not make adequate provision for the due observance of the Lord's Supper among the very people to whom he had taught his doctrine of 'Constant Communion'. During 1784-9, Wesley himself ordained twenty-seven Methodist preachers, but only three were to exercise their ministry in England. There can be little doubt that

---

[78] See Hymn No. 42.
[79] See Hymn No. 126, Archibald W. Harrison, *Church and Sacraments*, p. 69.

in this way he hoped to provide for the administration of the sacraments among his people after his death. But when that occurred, the Methodists refused to take a step which would have seemed to involve separation from the Church of England. At their first Conference they resolved to 'continue united to the Established Church, so far as the blessed work in which we are engaged will permit'. The next Conference was so divided on the subject that it was decided to determine the question 'by lot', the result being that for the next two years greater liberality in administration was allowed. The Methodists must either go to the parish church for the sacrament or do without it, except in London and a few other places where provision had been made. At last it became clear that the price of loyalty to the Established Church was the spiritual starvation of multitudes of Methodists. So in 1795, Conference passed the Plan of Pacification and permission was given for the observance of the Lord's Supper in Methodist chapels.

But the permission was hedged about by strange restrictions. It must not be administered in any place without the consent of the Conference or without the wish of the majority of the trustees and leaders. 'The Sacrament shall never be administered on those Sundays on which it is administered in the Parish Church.' For the same reason it was enacted that the Sacrament should be administered in Methodist chapels in the evening, in order to avoid 'Church hours' and the appearance of a rival altar. Thus there came into being a thing entirely new to Methodism—the Sunday evening Communion—and Wesley's wonderful morning sacramental services were entirely forgotten, and all this out of deference to the Church of England! 'The Methodists have paid a sad price for the pathetic loyalty of their fathers to their old, unkindly mother.'

Adam Clarke, in 1816, said: 'The Methodists in England have incomparably more grace and more stability since the introduction of the sacraments than before.' But the four years of prohibition which followed the death of Wesley and the restrictions of 1795 created a tradition which went far to annul the teaching and example of John Wesley and sowed seeds of which we reap the harvest even to this day.[80]

One of the early Methodist preachers, Thomas Taylor, writes: 'I was well aware that many of our people seldom went to Church, and received the Lord's Supper nowhere. Truly they had but sight of it; there might have been no such comment in the New Testament as "Do this in remembrance of Me".'[81] 'Our people have been exhorted to go to the Lord's Supper, but numbers are very ignorant of the nature and design of the solemn ordinance.'[82]

There were probably also psychological causes behind the decline of sacramental devotion in early nineteenth-century Methodism. The right to administer was given to all preachers in full connexion. These men were not ordained. This innovation must have been unacceptable to many because it was contrary to Wesley's belief and practice. When the Oxford Movement arose, the Methodists reacted against it, and this would cause a disparagement of the sacraments. Moreover, at the beginning of the nineteenth century Wesleyan Methodism had its love-feasts and class-meetings, which supplied some of the spiritual needs met by the Holy Communion. At the time, as Dr. Rattenbury points out: 'Methodism was hardening down into a separate denomination, and there would be a tendency perhaps to emphasize services which were sectarian and separatist in character rather than

---

[80] T. H. Barratt, op. cit. *London Quarterly Review*, July 1923.
[81] *Lives of Early Methodist Preachers*, Vol. V, p. 62.
[82] ibid., p. 73.

those which were Catholic and continuous with other Church life'.[83]

We are now in a position to examine the manner in which the Methodist Conference since the union of 1932 has given expression to the doctrine, evangelical, scriptural, and Wesleyan, which is implicit in its experience and explicit in its standards. Four authorities may be cited: The Standing Orders of the Conference, and the two orders of service for the administration of the Holy Communion and the Ordination Service authorized for use in the Methodist Church.

In the Standing Orders it is clearly stated that 'the Methodist Church recognizes two sacraments, namely, Baptism and the Lord's Supper, as of perpetual obligation, of which it is the privilege and duty of members of the Methodist Church to avail themselves'.[84] In addition, provision is made for all members to fulfil this obligation: 'Where, however, it can be shown that any church is deprived of a reasonably frequent and regular administration through lack of ministers, the circuit concerned may apply to Conference for the authorization of persons other than ministers to administer the sacrament.'

In both form of service authorized for use at the Holy Communion, the words used when the bread and wine are administered to the people are these:

'The Body of our Lord Jesus Christ, which was given for thee, preserve thee unto everlasting life. Take and eat this in remembrance that Christ died for thee, and feed on Him in thy heart by faith with thanksgiving.'

'The Blood of our Lord Jesus Christ, which was shed for thee, preserve thee unto everlasting life. Drink this in remembrance that Christ's Blood was shed for thee, and be thankful.'

Here is the association, if not the identification, of the

[83] *Wesley's Legacy to the World*, p. 192.   [84] Standing Order, No. 226.

bread and wine with the body and blood of our Lord, an association which is derived from Christ Himself. Here is the affirmation of the real presence of Christ, not in material form, but made evident through material means. Here the sacramental principle, vital to Christianity, is vindicated. Methodism does not limit the presence of Christ to Holy Communion; but it guarantees His presence to all who having repented of their sins, 'draw near with faith and take this holy sacrament to their comfort'.

In the Ordination Service the following question is put to each candidate:

'Will you then give your faithful diligence always so to minister the Doctrine and Sacraments, and the Discipline of Christ, as the Lord hath commanded?'

To which the candidate replies: 'I will do so, by the help of the Lord.' In loyalty to their ordination vows ministers must administer the Holy Communion and teach the doctrine which the Methodist Church has embodied in its standards. There is also provision for the ordinary Church member. Standing Orders lay down this regulation: 'Any member . . . who, without sufficient reason, persistently absents himself from the Lord's Supper, and from the meetings for Christian fellowship, shall be visited by both his leader and his minister. The names of any who by such prolonged absence sever themselves from Church membership, shall be removed by the Leaders' Meeting from the class book, and he shall thereupon cease to be a member of the Methodist Church.'[85] Provision is made for conscientious scruple, so that it cannot be said that membership depends upon sacramental observance alone.

The Communion Service of the Methodists, with a few variations, is that in use since 1662, substantially

[85] Standing Order, No. 225.

since 1549, in the Church of England. There is one significant alteration which, says T. H. Barratt, 'marks the watershed between the two great Oxford Movements, all the world of difference between Newman and Wesley'. In the Anglican order the minister says: 'Almighty God . . . pardon and deliver you from all your sins.' Wesley alters all the pronouns, and reads: 'Pardon and deliver us.' Other alterations that he made are: The phrase 'Ministers of Thy Gospel' was substituted for 'Bishops and Curates' in the Prayer for the Church Militant; two exhortations which are not parts of the service itself have been omitted; and the last exhortation leading up to the invitation 'Ye that do truly and earnestly repent' has been shortened.

In the latest revision of the Communion Office authorized by the Conference of 1936 there are some additions and omissions. In the Pre-Communion Service the Commandments of our Lord are printed for alternative use with the Ten Commandments, and the Collects for the King are omitted. In the Communion Service itself the words 'provoking most justly Thy wrath and indignation against us' are omitted from the Confession. To the Proper Prefaces is added one for All Saints' Day, a festival that was dear to the heart of John Wesley. In the prayer of Consecration the words 'oblation and satisfaction' are omitted after 'who made there by His one oblation of Himself a full, perfect, and sufficient sacrifice'. These words were originally inserted to affirm the all-sufficiency of Christ's finished work upon the Cross, and to contradict the claims of the Roman Church. The reason for their omission is that 'the historical protest has done its work, and the Eucharist, which is *sacramentum unitatis* should emphasize the agreements rather than the differences of Christian people'.[86] After the administration of the

[86] J. E. Rattenbury, *Vital Elements of Public Worship*, p. 140.

elements, a new rubric enjoins a period of silent prayer, after which the minister and all the people join in the Lord's Prayer. There is an alternative prayer of Thanksgiving printed after the prayer of Oblation. This latter is placed before Communion instead of after in the Deposited Prayer Book, and also in the alternative form of service authorized by the Methodist Conference, and there are good liturgical arguments for the position. But it is possible to read into the changed order the idea of sacrifice, and hence the reformers probably were wise to place it after Communion.

The present Order for the Communion Service is unique among the liturgies of those Churches which have retained the traditional or 'Catholic' shape of the Communion Office, in that it contains no reference to the Manual Acts. The last Methodist Service Book in which they appeared was *The Sunday Service of the Methodists* (1878). Here are the five rubrics inserted in the Prayer of Consecration:

'Who in the same night that he was betrayed, took bread (*a*) and when he had given thanks he break it (*b*) and gave it to his disciples saying, Take, eat; this (*c*) is my body which is given for you. . . . Likewise after supper, he took (*d*) the cup . . . saying, Drink ye all of this, for this (*e*) is my blood.'

(*a*) Here the minister is to take the paten into his hand.
(*b*) And here to break the bread.
(*c*) And here to lay his hand upon all the bread.
(*d*) Here he is to take the cup in his hand.
(*e*) And here to lay his hand upon the cup.

These simple but suggestive actions have been retained by the chief representatives of both Episcopal and Presbyterian Churches, and it is surprising that Methodism should have excised them from its service. The omission was not made by John Wesley and was not made until one hundred years after his death. There were no definite instructions for the performance of the Manual Acts in *The Book of Common Prayer* until the 1662 edition: the 1549 edition simply instructed the priest to take the bread and the cup into his hands. These were omitted at the 1552 revision, but restored in 1661.

It is difficult to say why the Manual Acts were left out of the 1882 edition of the *Methodist Service-Book*. 'There was at the time an anti-Anglican movement led by Dr. J. H. Rigg, which aimed at amending the Baptismal Service and removing traces of Anglican influence from the rest of the Service Book. There was alarm in some quarters at the supposed danger of Anglo-Catholic tendencies creeping into Wesleyan Methodism. In any case, several left-wing tendencies revealed themselves and the net result was that the Baptism service was amended, the Manual Acts omitted from the Communion Service, and three ministerial brethren seceded from the Connexion.'[87]

The Presbyterians have altered the service so that the Words of Institution, with three of the Manual Acts, do not occur within a prayer, but are read by the minister (see the *Scottish Book of Common Order*, 1928 edition, page 65). The idea behind this is that the minister standing behind the Table presents a re-enactment of the drama of the Upper Room. A parallel to the reformed order of service is to be found in the alternative order for Communion in the 1936 *Methodist Book of Offices* where the narrative of the Institution is read by the minister and is not contained within a prayer.

A good case can be made out for the restoration of the Manual Acts. They are in line with the best reformed

[87] John C. Bowmer, 'The Manual Acts in the Communion Office'; *London Quarterly and Holborn Review*, October 1945, p. 395.

tradition. Bernard Lord Manning has uttered a necessary warning against conceiving the Communion Service in such a way that 'those august and primitive actions which the Reformers were burnt to win for us from the confused millinery of the Mass are not now thought worth repeating'.[88] He points out that the Manual Acts are among the few actions which make the celebration. They are symbols which say what no words can utter. There is both a dramatic and a poetic value in the symbolic actions in the Communion Service, which it would be a pity to lose.

One characteristic of the Methodist observance of the Lord's Supper is that the communicants come to the Table in groups, not as solitary units. Thus an expression is given to the idea of the communion of saints. It is everywhere recognized that this communion is centred in the living presence of our Lord, who meets His own at the appointed trysting-place. This is Methodism's doctrine of the Real Presence. The Methodist is apt to be surprised at the individualism of the Anglican usage. He would agree with the verdict of Brilioth who says: 'The noble attempt of the *Prayer Book* of 1549 to make the Communion the central act of Divine worship was not followed up in the subsequent development of the liturgy, and it has been the great blot on the wonderful revival of sacramental religion in the Anglican communion that it has failed to recover the unity of Communion and Eucharist.'[89]

Another characteristic of the Methodist observance is that the Holy Communion has always been closely linked with the preaching of the Word, with its 'offer of Christ'. In consequence an open invitation is given to the Table of the Lord. All who will, may come, provided they love the Lord Jesus Christ in sincerity and truth. Dr. Adam Clarke expressed the intention when he said: 'Every minister of

---

[88] *Essays in Orthodox Dissent*, p. 55.
[89] *Eucharistic Faith and Practice*, p. 280.

Christ is bound to administer to every man who is seeking the salvation of his soul, as well as to believers.'

The Methodist minister is at liberty to 'use hymns and extempore prayer', but as the Communion Service usually follows another service the full rite is seldom used, let alone enriched by Wesley's sacramental hymns. This Sacrament, which unites the Methodist with Protestant and Catholic Christendom, is not given that high dignity which our tradition and our official utterances assign to it.

This study of the Methodist doctrine of the Holy Communion may fitly close with a definition from that great Methodist theologian of the last century, W. B. Pope: 'The Lord's Supper is a rite ordained by our Lord for perpetual observance in His Church, as a sacramental feast in which bread and wine are signs of His sacred body and blood, offered in one oblation on the Cross, and seals of the present and constant impartation to the believer of all the benefits of His Passion. This ordinance is the sacrament, as it signifies and seals the mystical nourishment of Christ: the Eucharist as commemorating the sacrifice of redemption: and the communion as the badge of united Christian profession.'[90]

HYMNS IN METHODIST WORSHIP

In a letter to which reference has already been made, written by John Wesley to a correspondent in Truro, he makes a comparison between the worship of the Established Church and that of the young Methodist societies, very much to the advantage of the latter. Having commented on the superior reverence in their case of both preacher and people he went on as follows:

'Nor are their solemn addresses to God interrupted

[90] *Compendium of Christian Theology*, Vol. III, p. 325.

either by the formal drawl of a parish clerk, the screaming of boys who bawl out what they neither feel nor understand, or the unseasonable and unmeaning impertinence of a voluntary on the organ. When it is seasonable to sing praise to God, they do it with the spirit and with the understanding also; not in the miserable, scandalous doggerel of Hopkins and Sternhold, but in psalms and hymns which are both sense and poetry, such as would sooner provoke a critic to turn Christian than a Christian to turn critic. What they sing is therefore a proper continuation of the spiritual and reasonable service, being selected for that end . . . by one who knows what he is about and how to connect the preceding with the following part of the service. Nor does he just take "two staves", but more or less, as may best raise the soul to God; especially when sung in well-composed and well-adapted tunes, not by a handful of wild, unawakened striplings, but by an whole serious congregation; and these not lolling at ease, or in the indecent posture of sitting, drawling out one word after another, but all standing before God, and praising Him lustily and with a good courage.'[91]

Wesley is certainly making the worst of what he criticizes. Yet much of the attraction of the movement he created and led consisted in the warmer and more enthusiastic conception of worship for which it stood and especially in the heart-felt participation of the whole congregation in that worship by means of a new and intimately personal type of hymnody.

Watts had vindicated the place of hymns in congregational worship, but the movement he inaugurated was purely liturgical. It was a deliberate attempt at the 'Renovation of Psalmody' in the ordinary worship of the Church. The revival methods of Wesley and his followers called for something different—a hymnody to reflect

[91] *Letters of John Wesley*, Vol. III, pp. 227-8.

the new kind of preaching initiated by them, a preaching that meant a bold appeal to each man's heart and conscience couched in popular language. When men's hearts are full their emotions clamour for utterance in speech and song and it was to their recognition of this simple psychological fact that a great part of the success of the pioneers of Methodism was due.

Dr. Dimond in his study of the psychology of the Methodist revival has pointed out that the mental condition desired in the congregation is akin to that induced by the romantic poet, who seeks to create in the minds of readers 'that willing suspension of disbelief for the moment, which constitutes poetic faith'.[92] In this condition the crowd was suggestible to a high degree. There is evidence that the hymns created in many the surprise and interest which is necessary if the state of 'poetic faith' is to be attained. The hymns also offered an opportunity of emotional expression by the people. In words which were understandable and with tunes sometimes taken from popular songs the congregation could express its penitence, its fears, its sorrows, and its joys.

Charles Wesley's hymns followed the order of the Church festivals and the holy days in the Christian Year, and thus used the old traditional festivals of English religious life as a guide to the devotion of the Methodist people. Before 1736, the Church of England had no hymn-book. The metrical versions of the Psalms by Sternhold and Hopkins or Tate and Brady were the only hymns available. So the congregational singing which the Wesleys introduced appealed to the common people because it was something entirely new. The hymns stimulated curiosity, and helped to create the attitude of wonder and surprise among those who heard them for the first time.

[92] *The Psychology of the Methodist Revival*, p. 117.

In the organization of the Revival itself, says Dr. Dimond, the hymns were of value in three directions. 'Their power of suggestion, their educational value, and the effect of the music with which they were associated contributed in a marked degree to the creation of the desired emotional experience, and to the permanent influence of the religious ideas and impulses which were the psychological centre and soul of the movement.'[93] The fact that the whole congregation could take part in the singing made the hymn a medium for the expression of the emotions aroused by the revival experiences, and at the same time the emotion was intensified by its expression. Thus it is that 'the hymn is especially valuable for both suggestion and auto-suggestion'.[94] While the people sang heartily in rhythmic phrases the ideas which the Wesleys wanted to impress upon their minds, each individual suggested them to himself, and passed on the suggestion to his neighbour. As the themes of the hymns were doctrinal and experimental, by singing them frequently the converts came to be familiar with a range of religious ideas which formed a basis for further instruction.

The month after his conversion Wesley paid a visit to the headquarters of the Moravians at Herrnhut where he attended a public service 'at which they frequently use other instruments with their organ. They began (as usual) with singing. Then followed the expounding, closed by a second hymn. Prayer followed this; and then a few verses of a third hymn, which concluded the service.'[95] The effect of this was still further to increase Wesley's enthusiasm for hymn-singing of the emotional type which was common among the Moravians. Such enthusiasm is

---

[93] ibid., p. 122.
[94] J. B. Pratt, *The Religious Consciousness*, p. 176.
[95] *Journal of John Wesley*, Vol. II, p. 20.

remarkable in a man of his temperament and training. But he found hymn-singing to be of practical value and therefore attached the utmost importance to it, not only for its use in exciting and expressing religious emotion, but also as a means of instruction and edification.

The Methodist hymns were to be a 'little body of experimental and practical divinity'. In his preface to the 1780 *Hymn-Book*, Wesley asks: 'In what other publication have you so distinct and full an account of scriptural Christianity, such a declaration of the heights and depths of religion, speculative and practical: so strong caution against the most plausible errors, particularly those now most prevalent, and so clear directions for making your calling and election sure, for perfecting holiness in the fear of God?' A century later, James Martineau, a thinker of a different type from Wesley, expressed the opinion of many competent judges of this work, when he said: 'After the Scriptures, the Wesley *Hymn-book* appears to me the grandest instrument of popular religious culture that Christendom has ever produced.'

From start to finish John and Charles Wesley were united by the closest bond of affection and by a profound community of ideas. 'Is there any other example of a great genius of John Wesley's eminence in leadership associated with another genius in a different mode of expression and forming such a powerful combination?'[96] The two brothers have been compared to Castor and Pollux, the great twin brethren who fought so well for Rome. Each with the other did rare exploits; neither without the other could have accomplished the mighty work which was wrought. John's was the brain which planned the Methodist hymnody, gave it its shape, made provision for it, encouraged its use, and recalled it to more sober paths when it degenerated into extravagance. The

[96] Sydney G. Dimond, op. cit., p. 120.

THE METHODIST CHURCH

poetical works of himself and his brother fill thirteen volumes. They first appeared in fifty-four volumes and booklets, from 1737 to 1790. Charles Wesley's poems and hymns may be generally regarded as giving the teaching of his brother John as well as his own. While Charles had a larger lyrical gift, John's taste was more severe and classical. He required hymns to be 'poetical', rational and scriptural. His own translations are numerous and of a high order. The power and beauty of the original are retained and are enriched by the purity and elegance of Wesley's rendering.

'Charles Wesley', says John Richard Green in his *History*, 'in his hymns expressed the fiery conviction of his converts in lines so chaste and beautiful that its more extravagant features disappeared. The wild throes of hysteric enthusiasm passed into a passion for hymn-singing, and a new musical impulse was aroused in the people which gradually changed the face of public devotion throughout England.'[97]

Charles Wesley's hymns have been described as a *Pilgrim's Progress* in song. Hardly anything in the eighteenth century before Blake can rival them in their richness of passion and language. They are far more intense and full of colour than the hymns of Watts, though necessarily more personal. The Tractarian Movement, for all its wealth of hymns, yielded nothing in quantity or general quality like the hymns of Methodism. John Keble's *The Christian Year* has neither the same vivacity nor range, either of subject or metre, for Charles Wesley has a hymn for every occasion. 'For light and life, force and fire, no hymns are to be compared to those of Charles Wesley. At times Watts may have surpassed them in calm grandeur of conception, and Doddridge in tenderness of sentiment, but beyond anything in either, there are in Charles

[97] *A Short History of the English People*, p. 738.

Wesley's hymns tones of conflict and victory which resemble the voice of a trumpet, and strains of praise like the sound of many waters.'[98]

Charles Wesley sets forth in song the whole range of the evangelical faith. It is a remarkable feat. Methodists have learned their doctrines from their hymns. By singing them they have not only got to know them, but to receive and approve them. Half of his six thousand hymns consist of well-considered and succinctly expressed comments upon some selected passage of Scripture. But beside those immediately founded upon a text, every hymn is steeped in Scripture metaphor and language. Take any hymn, examine it line by line, and it will be found that behind almost every expression lurks a word or image derived from the Bible. If Methodism has maintained its evangelical orthodoxy now for two centuries the fact is due not so much to John Wesley's sermons as to the influence of Charles's hymns. The reason is that the hymns presented Scripture or the doctrine, not as a truth or a dogma to be accepted, but as a glowing personal experience to be enjoyed.

A modern writer on hymnody says of Charles Wesley's hymns: 'Of many of them the ardent personal emotion is not for all tastes. In the ears of an undogmatic age their unashamed accent of evangelical Christianity may sound tiresome and out of date. Yet none the less, the religion they express has the authentic note of the Gospels and Epistles, and if ever the glow of early Methodism comes back to the English-speaking world, men will find no hymns more fitted to express it than the best of what Charles Wesley has bequeathed to them.'[99]

He wrote for all classes; for the society in all its meetings,

---

[98] John Stoughton, *Religion in England under Queen Anne and the Georges*, p. 400.
[99] C. S. Phillips, *Hymnody: Past and Present*, p. 183.

for children, for the Kingswood colliers, for condemned malefactors; he has hymns for the king and nation, for the great Christian festivals, for morning and evening, for daily work, for the sick-room, and for the hour of death. He uses in all some thirty metres and seems to be equally skilful with each.

At the time of the rise of Methodism the use of the hymn in church was a modern innovation confined to a few advanced Dissenters. So strong was the prejudice against these 'human hymns' as contrasted with the metrical 'Psalms of David', that even the paraphrases of Dr. Watts were looked upon with grave suspicion. The immediate popularity of Wesley's hymns may cause surprise. But it must be remembered that their use was confined to meetings which were not regarded as usurping the functions of public worship, and so raised no question of church order or propriety.

Soon after his return from Georgia in 1738, Wesley published *A Collection of Psalms and Hymns*. In 1741 he issued another volume (the third with the same title), which was used for nearly a century in the Methodist societies. After Wesley's death Dr. Coke published an enlarged edition of it, which the Conference of 1816 recommended 'for use in Methodist congregations in the forenoon'. Hence it was known as the 'Morning Hymn-book'. Most of the one hundred and sixty hymns in it are by Watts, and less than a quarter by the Wesleys. In 1753 Wesley published *Hymns and Spiritual Songs, Intended for the Use of Real Christians of all Denominations*. This book contained eighty-four hymns, mostly by Charles Wesley, and was in use in Methodist congregations until the publication of the large hymn-book in 1780.

So far no hymn-book had been published with tunes. To meet the demand for music as well as words, and to include some of his brother's latest hymns, in 1761, Wesley published *Select Hymns: with Tunes Annext. Designed Chiefly for the Use of the People called Methodists*. Still Charles continued to write and to publish new volumes of hymns, and at last in 1780 Wesley prepared another hymnal, making selections from the forty different hymn-books he had already published. For over a hundred years this remained the standard volume, though the *Morning Hymns* continued to be used.

Dr. Rattenbury has pointed out that this large hymn-book was a supplementary collection for a contingent society. It assumed the existence of the other hymn-books, containing Festival Hymns, Sacramental Hymns, Funeral Hymns, and the volume entitled *Psalms and Hymns*, all of which continued to be circulated separately even as late as 1830, until supplements made them redundant. This 1780 collection was not meant to be comprehensive: 'It was designed for a separate society which Wesley hoped would continue as such, but would at the same time retain its Church connexions. It never altogether satisfied the needs of that society. In Wesley's old age there were already men and forces in Methodism at work which claimed a full and separated Churchmanship and therefore required a hymn-book expressive of a wider religion than the contingent and supplementary teachings of distinctive Methodism. The more Methodism became independent of the Church of England the more it required a book which expressed the truths for which the Church stood as well as those of the distinctive Methodist Society. But Wesley thought otherwise and so deliberately made his book supplementary.'[100] In 1800 a supplement was added to the 1780 collection bringing up the number of hymns from 525 to 560, and including seven hymns on the Lord's Supper. In 1831 a further supplement was

[100] J. E. Rattenbury, *Evangelical Doctrine of Charles Wesley's Hymns*, p. 70.

added, making the total number of hymns 769. In this book 668 hymns are by the Wesleys.

In 1876 the Conference added another supplement containing 687 metrical psalms and hymns. This hymn-book continued in use in the Wesleyan Church till 1904, when it was recognized that another was required. In this the method of arrangement was entirely altered, and the usual theological order now found in hymnals was adopted. Many of Charles Wesley's hymns were omitted. Some three hundred new hymns were included in this collection of 981, most of which were by hymn-writers of the nineteenth century. This book in its turn was superseded after the Union of 1932 by another issued in 1933. Out of 984 hymns in the book, two hundred and ninety are those of Charles and twenty-six of John Wesley, together nearly one-third of the whole. Isaac Watts takes second place with forty-three hymns. In the preface to this latest book, it is claimed that this collection, like that of 1780, is primarily evangelical. 'It contains a large number of hymns which have proved their power both to deepen the spiritual life of believers and to inspire saving faith in Christ. . . . The claims of poetry have always been in mind, but those of religion have been paramount, and not a few hymns have been selected chiefly because they are dear to the people of God. For the one aim of every true hymn-book must be to "raise or quicken the spirit of devotion".'

It is interesting to study the Table of Contents of the 1780 collection. Its compiler says: 'The hymns are not carelessly jumbled together, but carefully ranged under proper heads, according to the experience of real Christians.' The book is divided into five parts. The first part is concerned with exhorting sinners to return to God. To this end it describes the pleasantness of religion, the goodness of God and the four Last Things: Death,

Judgement, Heaven, and Hell. The second part describes Formal Religion, which it contrasts with Inward Religion. The third part contains four sections: 1. Praying for repentance; 2. For mourners convinced of sin; 3. For persons convinced of backsliding; 4. For backsliders recovered. In the fourth part Wesley goes on to describe the experience of believers. He shows them rejoicing, fighting, praying, watching, working, suffering, seeking for full redemption, saved, and finally interceding for the world. In the last section Wesley considers his Society and provides them with hymns for their meetings, for giving thanks, for praying, and for parting. Dr. Dimond in his study of the psychology of the Methodist revival quotes this Table of Contents and then makes this comment: 'The emphasis on joy and praise, the elements of elation and self-expansion in Wesley's hymns have not received full recognition. The hymns are of great value as a record of the introspections and suggestions which have been used by the Methodist people from the early days of the movement.'[101]

Bernard Lord Manning has given the highest praise to this collection of hymns. He ranks it with the Psalms, *The Book of Common Prayer*, and the Canon of the Mass. 'In its own way, it is perfect, unapproachable, elemental in its perfection. You cannot alter it except to mar it; it is a work of supreme devotional art by a religious genius.' He names three features of the book which make it religiously great. 'There is the solid structure of historic dogma; there is the passionate thrill of present experience; and there is the glory of a mystic sunlight coming directly from another world.' These three qualities, he claims, give such a life to the hymns that they can never grow old while Christians experience God's grace.[102]

[101] op. cit., p. 121.
[102] *Hymns of Wesley and Watts*, pp. 14, 29.

The first Methodist tune-book was issued by Wesley in 1742 and was entitled: *A Collection of Tunes Set to Music, as they are Commonly Sung at the Foundery*. This 'Foundery' was situated near Moorfields, and had been used by the Government for casting cannon. After an explosion there in 1716 the place was abandoned, and remained in ruins till 1739, when Wesley bought it and turned it into the first Methodist meeting-house in London.

Wesley's experience of the bad singing of the old psalm-tunes led him to exclude all but three of them from his tune-book. But the newer psalm-tunes, like HANOVER readily find a place. Fourteen of the forty tunes of this collection are of German origin. Wesley became acquainted with the German chorales through his association with the Moravians. The 'Foundery Tune-Book' was one of the worst printed books ever issued from the Press, and it was full of mistakes. Toward the end of 1746 the first book of original tunes to Charles Wesley's hymns appeared under the title of *Hymns on the Great Festivals, and other Occasions*. This was the work of John F. Lampe, a bassoon player and writer of opera, converted under Charles Wesley, who took to writing music for the Methodists.

For the next few years the tunes used by the Methodists consisted of those from the 'Foundery Book' and many of Lampe's, and original compositions and local melodies that John Wesley met with in his travels. The singing of the Methodists was becoming noted, not only for its heartiness, but for the attractive tunes they used. In 1761 Wesley published a second and worthier tune-book, entitled *Sacred Melody*, and containing one hundred and fifteen tunes. About a third of the tunes are in the minor scale. 'Many of these have virility and jubilant qualities, but they were peculiarly calculated to kindle the emotions of awe and wonder and an attitude of repentance and

150   METHODIST WORSHIP

hope.'[103] Few of the psalm-tunes were inserted into this collection, probably because the Methodist meeting was a supplement to the Church worship. There are a number of tunes from German sources, and arrangements from Handel, Purcell, Arne, and other composers of the period. Secular melodies were freely used. Charles Wesley said that he did not see why the devil should have all the good tunes and so he took some of the popular airs of his day and wedded them to his words. The story of how, in order to win some drunken sailors who were singing a popular song of the music-hall called 'Nancy Dawson', he wrote a hymn to fit the tune is well known. At the time of the great earthquake he composed 'He comes, He comes, the judge severe', to be sung to a well-known patriotic song by Carey: 'He comes, he comes, the hero comes.'[104]

In the preface to *Sacred Melody*, John Wesley said: 'This collection contains all the tunes in common use among us. They are pricked true, exactly as I desire all our congregations may sing them.' This statement is important for it establishes the fact that the real 'old Methodist tunes' are those contained in the various editions of this book, and not the florid and repeating tunes that often pass under that name.[105] The title *Sacred Melody* is derived from the fact that only the air of each tune is given; but after it had been in use for many years Wesley decided to issue a harmonized edition, and in 1781 his last tune-book appeared. This is known as *Sacred Harmony* and contains the tunes arranged for two or three voices, and also the hymns to each tune.

Wesley's directions for using his tune-book from the preface to *Sacred Melody* are worth reproducing.

[103] Sydney G. Dimond, op. cit., p. 123.
[104] *New History of Methodism*, Vol. II, pp. 557-62.
[105] J. T. Lightwood, *Hymn-Tunes and Their Story*, p. 136.

'1. Learn these Tunes before you learn any others; afterwards learn as many as you please.

'2. Sing them exactly as they are printed here, without altering or mending them at all; and if you have learned to sing them otherwise, unlearn it as soon as you can.

'3. Sing All. See that you join with the congregation as frequently as you can. Let not a slight degree of weakness or weariness hinder you. If it is a cross to you, take it up, and you will find it a blessing.

'4. Sing lustily and with a good courage. Beware of singing as if you were half dead or half asleep; but lift up your voice with strength. Be no more afraid of your voice now, nor more ashamed of its being heard, than when you sung the songs of Satan.

'5. Sing modestly. Do not bawl, so as to be heard above or distinct from the rest of the congregation, that you may not destroy the harmony; but strive to unite your voices together, so as to make one clear melodious sound.

'6. Sing in Time. Whatever tune is sung, be sure to keep with it. Do not run before nor stay behind it; but attend close to the leading voices, and move therewith as exactly as you can; and take care not to sing too slow. This drawling way very naturally steals on all who are lazy; and it is high time to drive it out from among us, and sing all our tunes just as quiet as we did at first.

'7. Above all, sing spiritually. Have an eye to God in every word you sing. Aim at pleasing Him more than yourself, or any other creature. In order to do this attend strictly to the sense of what you sing, and see that your heart is not carried away with the sound, but offered to God continually. So shall your singing be such as the Lord will approve of here, and reward you when He cometh in the clouds of heaven.'

It was the practice to 'line out' the hymns at the services, two lines at a time, and not more than three hymns were permitted at any one service. The Methodists stood to sing. The men and women, ranged on opposite sides of the building, were encouraged to sing their own part. Every effort was made to get everyone present to sing with intelligence and heartiness. New tunes were only introduced when the old ones were known. Anthems were not allowed and the use of instruments was rare. The introduction of organs in the early part of the nineteenth century was the cause of much bitter contention and led finally to a schism. But Methodist singing proved a great attraction, as is evidenced by the testimony of a clergyman, William Vincent, later Dean of Salisbury, at the end of the eighteenth century who said: 'For one who has been drawn away from the Established Church by preaching, ten have been induced by music.'[106] The heightening of emotion by means of the music was one of the most effective agencies in creating the atmosphere in which conversions were to be expected.

The number of hymn-writers in the Evangelical Revival is amazing, and the permanence of their songs is a remarkable fact. Besides Watts and Doddridge, an honourable place must be given to Edward Perronet, a companion of Charles Wesley in his itinerant days who composed 'All hail the power of Jesu's name'; to John Cennick, one-time master at Wesley's school at Kingswood, who will be remembered for his evening hymn 'Ere I sleep', and for 'Thou great Redeemer, dying Lamb'; to John Bakewell, a Methodist class-leader, and author of 'Hail, thou once despised Jesus'; to Thomas Olivers, the composer of 'The God of Abraham praise'; and to many another. The Revival brought hymn-singing into the churches, produced hymn-books, and enriched for ever the hymnology of the Church.

Let Evelyn Underhill, a writer of a very different school,

[106] *Considerations on Parochial Music*, pp. 10, 14.

pay her tribute to the influence of Methodist hymns. 'They spread through England the forgotten treasure of Christian spirituality, though expressed in language which the simplest worshipper could understand. In them we find reminiscences of all the masters of adoring worship, Catholic and Protestant alike; from St. Augustine to the Quietists. . . . In the greatest of these hymns, especially those of Charles Wesley, we can recognize the fervour and realism which swept the country to rekindle the smouldering devotional life. They constitute the true liturgy of Methodism; and in them, as in other liturgies, the essential spirit can still be found. They were, and are, greatly used both in public worship and private devotion; and although their exalted temper hardly represents the average religious level they have taught the deep secrets of communion with God to a multitude of humble saints.'[107]

[107] *Worship*, pp. 305-6.

Epilogue

THE Free Churches still have a vital contribution to make to the life of Christ's Church. Dr. Barry, the Bishop of Southwell, in a recent book, admits that the Church of England has much to learn from the Free Churches. 'It is plain', he says, 'that it is now necessary to supplement the existing forms of worship with a considerable amount of new matter which is frankly topical and contemporary.' He points out that the Free Churches have preserved something very precious in the value that they set upon extempore prayer, using the word 'extempore' to mean, not 'unprepared', but 'relevant to the immediate situation'. Its religious importance is its topicality. It is not traditional, but experimental. 'As in recent years the Free Church has borrowed much from Anglican Service-books, so they have now this gift to bring to us. What our Church needs today is the marriage of the liturgical with the experimental.'[1]

The Anglican contribution of belief in an historic Church and in a corporate devotional life needs to be corrected by the Free Church emphasis on democratic fellowship and elasticity, so that worship may be kept human by constant contact with the changing world. The public worship of God is a high and holy thing, and it is not to be attained without consecrated effort on the part of all those who engage in it. The Free Churches cannot discharge their mission by becoming pale imitations of other Churches, but only by being themselves and living up to their ideals.

It would be foreign to the genius of the Free Church to

[1] *Church and Leadership*, p. 108.

seek a rigid form of service. But there is a rough framework in the typical form which unites them with the Christian Church worshipping through the ages and it would be well for them to recognize and respect it, and use it with a pliancy natural to Churches which claim to be free.

The recent tendency in the Free Churches has been to exercise their freedom to use or not to use liturgical forms of prayer as occasion requires. This freedom has sometimes been used without sufficient regard to the essential elements of Christian worship, whether in respect of the truth presented to the worshipper or of the response asked of him. The Gospel has not always been presented in its wholeness, nor has the Christian pattern of response in adoration, penitence, thanksgiving, and the acceptance of deliverance been effectively reproduced.

In a recent statement on *Christian Worship—Decline and Recovery*, issued by the Free Church Fellowship, this criticism is passed on modern Free Church practice. 'The average Sunday service of Free Church worship is hardly to be described as a Communion in the Body and Blood of Christ; a tasting of the powers of the New Age; a recognition that in Christ the Kingdom of God has come among us; a covenant with Him to share His conflict with the existing order of things; an occasion for the sure reception of the power of His Resurrection to judge and overthrow the citadels of evil in our midst. It tends to decline to a more prosaic level on which it is enough if we find encouragement in the consolations of the Gospel, forgiveness for the sins of the past week and renewal of the aspiration after a more Christian way of living—a good thing indeed, but how far from the terrifying splendour of the new life promised in the Gospel to the true Church of Jesus Christ.'[2]

[2] Leaflet No. 108, p. 4.

This condition of things points clearly to the urgent need of a work of education in the hearts and minds of all who worship. Public worship is an art, and an art has always to be learned. It cannot be really effective unless there be in the hearts of the worshippers a conception of God which is vital, vivid, spiritual, and above all awe-inspiring.

How are we to awaken in the hearts and minds of the congregation a realization of the tremendous character of Christian worship? This result may be attained in many ways. The spirit of worship may be quickened and its expression enriched by the introduction into the services of the wealth of devotional literature which is the common heritage of all the Churches. All the non-liturgical denominations are making a definite effort to lift public worship to a higher level. Nowhere is any tendency to uniformity apparent. None of the denominations has brought any pressure to bear to ensure conformity to the forms of service it has published, but merely offers them as suggestions or recommendations.

It is by no means certain that the Free Churches by denuding their buildings of all external aids to worship have secured a real interiority. External objects sometimes assist those who pray confronting them. It is surely a mistake to ban God's gift of beauty and colour from His house and to ignore the way in which the eye affects the heart. There is need in the Free Churches for the appeal through 'eye-gate' as well as 'ear-gate'. Evelyn Underhill reminds us that 'because men are creatures of sense as well as spirit, of body as well as soul, we must bring our senses and our bodies in, and let them play their part in the worshipping act; eye and ear are veritable channels through which our sense-conditioned spirits can receive messages from God and respond to Him.'[3] Symmetry

[3] *Collected Papers*, p. 67.

of structure, grace of form, harmony in colouring and taste in ornamentation can awaken the emotions and incite to worship.

Other means of bringing home to the worshippers the true character of Christian worship are—the more frequent use of the great objective hymns which clearly affirm the faith; the more regular exposition of the essentials of Christian worship; the more balanced selection of sermon themes so that the whole counsel of God is declared, and the better observance of the Christian Year. The worshipper needs to be trained so that he is aware of the purpose of all the different items in the service and of the response expected of him to each. That response must be such as he can fully understand; therefore it is desirable that there should be a recognized structure in a service which is familiar to leader and people.

If the Free Churches are to make a national appeal, they must make religious provision for every type of spiritual need. At present they are not catholic enough in their forms of devotion. There is need for variety and flexibility in worship. The spiritual life of the individual Christian and of the whole Church requires various habits of devotion if it is to be rightly nourished. Public worship must not only be adequate to the fullness of the Christian Gospel, but also to the whole of life as men have to live it. It is not surprising if there is discontent with forms of worship that appear to be too narrow in their range or too rigidly ordered.

A distinguished scholar has said that 'the ritualist and the puritan conceptions of worship will probably exist side by side, for they represent two opposite conceptions of religion which can never entirely blend'.[4] Doubtless it is true that there are two opposite conceptions

[4] Dill, *Roman Society from Nero*, p. 603.

of religion, but they can be complementary instead of antagonistic. If the ritualist could learn the truth which the puritan asserts, and the puritan become aware of what the ritualist means, the foundation would be laid for the universal Church. 'The peril of Protestantism is individualism: the peril of Catholicism is institutionalism.'[5] The Protestant outlook makes worship the expression of what man knows of God's will and grace; the Catholic view makes worship the instrument for creating the sense of God's grace and the appreciation of His presence. But these are not ultimately contradictory, for in actual worship complete objectivity or complete subjectivity is rarely found. It is clear that both the objective and the subjective, the corporate and the individualistic, are needed in Christian worship. What is to be desired and striven for is a balanced worship which possesses the excellences of both tendencies and is not narrowed by the exclusion of either.

[5] cf. D. H. Hislop, *Our Heritage in Public Worship*, p. 335; and J. E. Rattenbury, *Vital Elements in Public Worship*, p. 76.

BIBLIOGRAPHY

ALLEN, A. V. G., *Christian Institutions* (T. and T. Clark).

ARTHUR, WILLIAM, *The Tongue of Fire* (Epworth Press).

BARBOUR, G. F., *Life of Alexander Whyte* (Hodder and Stoughton).

BARRATT, T. H., 'The Place of the Lord's Supper in Early Methodism', *London Quarterly and Holborn Review*, July 1923 (Epworth Press).

BARRY, F. R., *Church and Leadership* (S.C.M. Press).

BETT, HENRY, *The Spirit of Methodism* (Epworth Press).

——*The Hymns of Methodism* (Epworth Press).

BLACK, JAMES, *The Mystery of Preaching* (James Clarke).

BOWMER, J. C., 'The Manual Acts in the Communion Office', *London Quarterly and Holborn Review*, October 1945 (Epworth Press).

BRILIOTH, YNGRE, *Eucharistic Faith and Practice, Evangelical and Catholic* (S.P.C.K. Press).

BROWN, JOHN, *Puritan Preaching in England*.

BUNTING, T. P., *Life of Jabez Bunting*, 2 Vols. (Longmans, Green).

BYINGTON, E. H., *The Quest for Experience in Worship* (New York).

CAIRNS, FRANK, *The Prophet of the Heart* (Hodder and Stoughton).

COCKS, H. LOVELL, 'The Place of the Sermon in Worship,' *Expository Times*, Vol. 49.

COLE, R. LEE, *Lovefeasts* (Kelly).

COLEMAN, T. W., *The Free Church Sacrament and Catholic Ideals* (Dent).

COOMER, DUNCAN, *English Dissent Under the Early Hanoverians* (Epworth Press).

DAKIN, A., *Calvinism* (Duckworth).

DAVIES, HORTON, *The Worship of the English Puritans* (Dacre Press).

DEARMER, PERCY, *The Church at Prayer* (James Clarke).

DENNEY, JAMES, *The Church and the Kingdom* (Hodder and Stoughton).
DIMOND, S. G., *The Psychology of the Methodist Revival* (Epworth Press).
DODD, C. H., *The Apostolic Preaching and its Developments* (Hodder and Stoughton).
DRUMMOND, A. L., *The Church Architecture of Protestantism* (T. and T. Clark).
DYKES, J. O., *The Christian Minister and His Duties* (T. and T. Clark).
EAYRS, TOWNSEND and WORKMAN: *New History of Methodism*, 2 vols. (Hodder and Stoughton).
EDWARDS, M. L., *After Wesley* (Epworth Press).
—— *Methodism and England* (Epworth Press).
FARMER, H. H., *The Servant of the Word* (Nisbet).
FLEMINGTON, W. F., *The New Testament Doctrine of Baptism* (S.P.C.K. Press).
—— 'The Holy Communion', in *Prayer and Worship*, Cambridge University Sermons (Hodder and Stoughton).
FORSYTH, P. T., *Positive Preaching and the Modern Mind* (Independent Press).
GARVIE, A. E., *The Christian Preacher* (T. and T. Clark).
GILLMAN, F. J., *The Evolution of the English Hymn* (Allen and Unwin).
GRAYSTON, KENNETH, 'On the Order of Service for the Baptism of Infants', *London Quarterly and Holborn Review*, July 1944 (Epworth Press).
GREGORY, A. S., *Praises with Understanding* (Epworth Press).
GREGORY, BENJAMIN, *Sidelights on the Conflicts of Methodism, 1898: Autobiographical Recollections* (Hodder and Stoughton).
HARRISON, A. W., *Church and Sacraments* (Epworth Press).
HISLOP, D. H., *Our Heritage in Public Worship* (T. and T. Clark).
HUNTER, FREDERICK, *Wesley Historical Society Proceedings*, June 1940, June and December 1942 (Epworth Press).
JACKSON, THOMAS, *Life of Robert Newton* (John Mason).
JAMES, A. GORDON, 'The Methodist Doctrine of Holy Communion', *London Quarterly and Holborn Review*, January 1940 (Epworth Press).

BIBLIOGRAPHY 161

JOWETT, J. H., *The Preacher, His Life and Work* (Hodder and Stoughton).
LEE, UMPHREY, *John Wesley and Modern Religion* (Abingdon-Cokesbury Press, Nashville).
LIGHTWOOD, J. T., *Hymn Tunes and Their Story* (Epworth Press).
MANNING, BERNARD L., *Essays in Orthodox Dissent* (Independent Press).
—— *The Hymns of Wesley and Watts* (Epworth Press).
MICKLEM, E. R., *Our Approach to God* (Hodder and Stoughton).
MICKLEM, NATHANAEL, *The Creed of a Christian* (S.C.M. Press).
—— Ed. *Christian Worship* (Oxford University Press).
MILLIGAN, O. B., *The Ministry of Worship* (Hodder and Stoughton).
MUMFORD, NORMAN W., 'The Administration of the Sacrament of Baptism in the Methodist Church', *London Quarterly and Holborn Review*, April 1947 (Epworth Press).
PECK, D. G., *Living Worship* (Eyre and Spottiswoode).
PHILLIPS, C. S., *Hymnody Past and Present* (S.P.C.K.).
PIETTE, MAXIMIN, *John Wesley in the Evolution of Protestantism* (Sheed and Ward).
POPE, W. B., *A Compendium of Christian Theology*, 3 vols. (Wesleyan Conference Office).
PRATT, J. B., *The Religious Consciousness* (Macmillan).
RATTENBURY, J. E., *Wesley's Legacy to the World* (Epworth Press).
—— *Vital Elements in Public Worship* (Epworth Press).
—— *The Conversion of the Wesleys* (Epworth Press).
—— *The Evangelical Doctrine of Charles Wesley's Hymns* (Epworth Press).
—— *The Eucharistic Hymns of John and Charles Wesley* (Epworth Press).
RUPP, E. GORDON, Essay in *The Holy Communion: A Symposium* (S.C.M. Press).
RUTHERFORD, MARK, *Autobiography* (Oxford University Press).
SCLATER, J. R. P., *The Public Worship of God* (Hodder and Stoughton).
SCOTT, A. BOYD, *Preaching Week by Week* (Hodder and Stoughton).

SCOTT, C. ANDERSON, *The Church, its Worship and Sacraments* (S.C.M. Press).
SIMON, J. S., *John Wesley: The Last Phase* (Epworth Press).
SIMPSON, R. S., *Ideas in Corporate Worship* (T. and T. Clark).
SMITH, C. RYDER, *The Sacramental Society* (Epworth Press).
SPERRY, WILLIAM L., *Reality in Worship* (Macmillan).
SPURGEON, C. H., *Lectures to My Students:* First Series. (Alabaster and Passmore).
STEWART, G. S., *The Lower Levels of Prayer* (S.C.M. Press)
STEWART G. WAUCHOPE, *Music in Church Worship* (Hodder and Stoughton).
STREETER, B. H., Ed. *Concerning Prayer* (Macmillan).
STOUGHTON, JOHN, *Religion in England Under Queen Anne and the Georges.*
TYERMAN, LUKE, *Life and Times of John Wesley*, 3 vols. (Hodder and Stoughton).
UNDERHILL, EVELYN, *Worship* (Nisbet).
——*Collected Papers* (Longmans, Green).
WATTS, ISAAC, *Works of Isaac Watts* (Independent Press).
——*The Lives of the Early Methodist Preachers* (John Mason).
WESLEY, JOHN, *John Wesley's Journal*, Standard Edition (Epworth Press).
——*John Wesley's Letters*, Standard Edition (Epworth Press).
——*John Wesley's Sermons*, Standard Edition (Epworth Press).
——*John Wesley's Works*, 10th Edition (Epworth Press).

INDEX OF AUTHORS

ALLEINE, RICHARD AND JOSEPH, 107-10
Allen, A. V. G., 57
Arthur, William, 35
Augustine, St., 17, 40

BARRATT, T. H., 124f., 131f.
Barry, F. R., 154
Beethoven, 22
Bett, Henry, 86
Black, James, 31, 43
Bowmer, J. C., 136f.
Brevint, Dr., 127-8
Bridges, Robert, 21
Brilioth, Yngve, 137
Brown, Dr. John, 46-7
Bruce, Robert, 56
Bunsen, Baron, 41
Bunting, Jabez, 91-4
Byington, E. H., 44

CAIRNS, FRANK, 49
Calvin, 72, 122
Clarke, Adam, 91, 94, 131, 137
Cocks, H. F. Lovell, 53
Cole, R. Lee, 103
Coleman, T. W., 68
Crowther, B., 104

DAKIN, A., 122
Davies, Horton, 104
Dearmer, Percy, 51
Denney, James, 43, 50
Dimond, S. G., 140-2, 148, 150
Dodd, C. H., 47, 69
Drummond, A. L., 6
Dykes, J. O., 59, 72, 75

FARMER, H. H., 21, 50
Forsyth, P. T., 48, 52, 65, 74

GILLMAN F. J., 17
Gore, Bishop, 12
Grayston, K., 116-19
Green, John Richard, 143
Gregory, A. S., 23

HISLOP, D. H., 42, 55, 158
Hughes, H. Price, 98
Hunter, Frederick, 88-90, 109

JACKSON, THOMAS, 95
James, A. Gordon, 121f.
Johnson, Dr. Samuel, 39
Jowett, J. H., 33

KNOX, ALEXANDER, 79

LIGHTWOOD, J. T., 150
Luther, Martin, 9-10, 24, 52, 64, 73

MANNING, B. L., 17-18, 137, 148
Martineau, James, 142
Micklem, E. R., 76
Micklem, Nathanael, 64
Milligan, O. B., 49, 72
Milton, John, 23
Mumford, N. W., 121

NEWMAN, J. H., 29, 55
Newton, John, 18
Newton, Robert, 94

OWEN, JOHN, 36, 70, 129

PATER, WALTER, 77
Pawson, John, 126
Peck, D. G., 12
Phillips, C. S., 19, 144
Piette, Maximin, 78
Pope, W. B., 119, 122, 138
Pratt, J. B., 4-7, 51, 141

RATTENBURY, J. E., 78, 86, 98, 131, 134, 146, 158
Rupp, E. G., 121
Rutherford, Mark, 38

SCLATER, J. R. P., 14, 61, 72
Scott, A. Boyd, 54
 C. Anderson, 58, 62
Secker, Thomas, 125
Simon, John, 84

Smith, C. Ryder, 63
Spenser, Edmund, 12
Sperry, W. L., 7, 13, 15, 34
Spurgeon, C. H., 34
Stewart, G. S., 36
Stoughton, John, 144
Streeter, B. H., 11, 29, 39, 66
Sugden, E. H., 114-15

TAYLOR, THOMAS, 131
Tennyson, Alfred, 18
Tersteegen, 16
Troeltsch, E., 81
Tunbridge, W. J., 96
Tyerman, Luke, 79, 83, 88

UNDERHILL, EVELYN, 3, 20, 30, 153, 156
VINCENT, WM., 152

WALKER, SAMUEL, 81, 89
Watson, Richard, 95
Watts, Isaac, 37, 139, 143, 145, 147
Wesley, John, 19, 21, 78-89, 101-29, 138-51 *passim*
  Charles, 22, 67, 70, 107, 113, 128, 140, 142-52
Whyte, Alexander, 27
Will, R., 11
Williamson, Wallace, 30

ZWINGLI, 66, 122

INDEX OF SUBJECTS

AMERICAN METHODISM, 84-6, 125

BAPTISM, 58ff, 111ff.
Bible, the, 6, 37, 41ff.

CATHOLIC WORSHIP CONTRASTED WITH PROTESTANT, 4-7, 50, 57, 158
Church of England, the, 31, 33, 48-9, 59, 72, 79ff., 101, 125, 130, 137
Communion Holy, 28, 66ff., 87, 121ff.
Covenant Service, 107-11

EXTEMPORE PRAYER, 32-6

FORM IN WORSHIP, 11ff., 35, 157

HYMNS, 17ff., 99, 128-9, 138ff.

LECTIONARY, USE OF, 45
Lessons, reading of, 41ff.
Liturgical prayer, 28-32, 91ff.
Love-feast, 102-4
Lutheran worship, 9-10

MANUAL ACTS AT HOLY COMMUNION, 75, 135

Moravians, the, 102, 105-6, 141
Music in worship, 21ff.

OFFICES, BOOK OF, 60, 96, 99, 114, 116, 119, 123, 134ff.

PACIFICATION, PLAN OF, 90, 93, 120, 130
Prayer, Book of Common, 31, 84ff., 91-6, 114, 116ff., 134
Presbyterians, 8, 39, 45, 61, 72, 88, 91, 108, 136
Puritans, English, 103-4

REFORMATION, THE, 2, 9, 42, 50, 73, 78, 100

SACRAMENTS, THE, 55ff.
Sermon, 46ff., 73
Silence, use of, 40
Synagogue worship, 3-4, 41

TEMPLE WORSHIP, 3-4
Tunes, hymn, 21ff, 146ff.

WATCHNIGHT SERVICE, 105-7

YEAR THE CHRISTIAN, 30, 45, 54, 98, 140, 157